Steck Vaughn

Maps Globes Graphs

Contents

Meet your state standards with free blackline masters and links to other materials at
www.HarcourtAchieve.com/AchievementZone.
Click Steck-Vaughn Standards.

ISBN 0-7398-9111-1

© 2004 Harcourt Achieve Inc.

Harcourt Achieve
Rigby · Steck-Vaughn

www.HarcourtAchieve.com
1.800.531.5015

About the Program

Steck-Vaughn *Maps•Globes•Graphs* has been developed to teach important geography and social studies skills in a six-level program. Up-to-date, in-depth information in a self-contained format makes this series an ideal supplement to basal texts or an excellent independent social studies skills course. Clear, concise maps present new concepts in a straightforward manner without overwhelming students with too much information. As students develop practical skills, such as map interpretation, they also develop the confidence to use these skills. The features incorporated into the *Maps•Globes•Graphs* program were developed to achieve these goals.

Maps•Globes•Graphs consists of six student books with accompanying annotated Teacher's Editions. The series is organized as follows:

Book	Level
Level A	Grade 1
Level B	Grade 2
Level C	Grade 3
Level D	Grade 4
Level E	Grade 5
Level F	Grade 6

STUDENT EDITION FEATURES

◆ **Consistent formats** for each chapter include two teaching pages that introduce the skill, two practice pages, one mixed practice page, and *Skill Check*, a review page.

◆ **Geography Themes Up Close** introduces the five themes of geography—location, place, human/environment interaction, movement, and regions—in the beginning of the book. These themes are reinforced in five two-page special features that emphasize the concepts and relevance of the themes.

◆ *Map Attack!* and *Graph Attack!* features (in the three upper-grade books) build general understanding of interpreting map and graph information in a step-by-step format.

◆ **Vocabulary** words highlighted in bold type emphasize in-context definitions and increase understanding of the terms critical to studies in geography.

◆ **Glossaries** in each student book serve as both an index and a resource for definitions of key terms.

◆ **Atlas maps** in each book are a valuable reference tool for instruction and study.

TEACHER EDITION FEATURES

◆ **Annotated** Teacher's Editions facilitate effective instruction with minimal preparation.

◆ **Scope and Sequence** reflects key concepts of basal instruction for each grade level.

◆ **Teaching strategies** identify key objectives and vocabulary for each chapter and provide suggestions for introducing skills, teaching specific lesson pages and concepts, following up lessons with extension activities, and enhancing concept mastery with activities to complete at home.

◆ **Extension activities** involve both cooperative learning and critical thinking, and reinforce the concepts and skills taught in the program.

◆ **Geography themes teaching strategies** reinforce geography skills and vocabulary through lesson introductions, teaching notes, and extension activities.

◆ **Blackline Masters** further supplement the activities available for use:

Map Attack! may be used with maps in a basal text or in reference materials.

Outline maps appropriate to each grade level may be used for skills practice in map labeling and place recognition.

Activities and *games* reinforce concepts.

Standardized tests in each level allow students to check their learning, as well as practice test-taking skills.

Steck-Vaughn Company grants you permission to duplicate enough copies of these blacklines to distribute to your students. You can also use these blacklines to make overhead transparencies.

◆ **Transparencies** provide full-color instructional aids. These transparencies may be used to introduce lessons, to reinforce key map and globe skills, or to review chapter concepts. These transparencies are perforated in the back of the teacher's editions for easy removal.

◆ **Letters to Families,** in English and in Spanish, are provided in each book. The letters invite families to participate in their child's study of the book and provide suggestions for some specific activities that can extend the concepts presented in the program.

SUGGESTIONS FOR PROGRAM USE

Maps•Globes•Graphs is easy to implement in any classroom. The following suggestions offer ways to adapt the program to particular classroom and student needs.

◆ Alternate the *Maps•Globes•Graphs* chapters with chapters in the social studies program. After presenting your first social studies chapter, present the first chapter of *Maps•Globes•Graphs*. When you return to the regular social studies program, apply any map skills learned to maps that appear in the curriculum. In this way, students reinforce their new skills in a variety of contexts.

◆ Set aside a specific time each week for map study. For example, spend half an hour every Friday on map study. Do as much in the *Maps•Globes•Graphs* Worktext® as time permits. Related activities, such as map show and tell, could be included in the map study time.

◆ Focus on a complete chapter of map study and cover the entire program at the beginning of the year, at the end of the year, or whenever best fits your class schedule.

The map and globe chapters in *Maps•Globes•Graphs* progress developmentally. For this reason they should be taught in the order they are presented in the Worktext®. However, the last chapter in each book presents several types of graphs, so this chapter could be interspersed with map chapters. In Levels D, E, and F, the graph topics reflect subjects covered by the maps and the basal programs. The graphs also can be used in conjunction with the graph presentation in mathematics studies.

Meet your state standards with free blackline masters and links to other materials at **www.HarcourtAchieve.com/AchievementZone**. Click **Steck-Vaughn Standards**.

Scope and Sequence

Numbers refer to the chapters where each skill is first taught. These skills are reviewed and reinforced throughout the book and the series, as well as in the "Geography Themes Up Close" special features.

		LEVEL A	LEVEL B	LEVEL C	LEVEL D	LEVEL E	LEVEL F
Map Recognition	Photo/Picture Distinction	1, 2					
	Photo/Map Distinction	3	2	1			
	Map defined	3	2	1	1		2
Map Key/Legend	Pictorial symbols/Symbol defined	6	2	1	1	2	
	Labels	7	7	1	1	2	2
	Legend defined and related to map	6	2	1	1	2	2
	Abstract symbols		2, 3, 6	1, 3	1	2	2
	Political boundaries		6	1	1	2	2
Direction	Top, Bottom, Left, Right	4					
	North, South, East, West	5	3	1	1	1	1
	Relative location	4–7	3–6	1–6	1–8	1–5, 7, 8, 11	2–5, 10
	Compass rose		3	1	1	1	2
	Cardinal directions (term)				1	1	2
	Intermediate directions			1	2	1	2
Scale and Distance	Miles/Kilometers/Map Scale/Distance			2	4	3	3
	Mileage markers				5	4	4
Latitude and Longitude	Equator		4	7	7	8	1, 6
	Latitude			7	7	8	6
	Degrees			7, 8	7	8	6
	Longitude/Prime Meridian			8	8	9	6
	Estimating Degrees				7	8, 9	6
	Parallel					8	6
	Meridian					9	6
	Latitude and Longitude					9	6
The Globe	Globe	7	4	7, 8	7, 8	1	1
	North Pole/South Pole		4	8	7, 8	1, 8–10	1
	Continents/Oceans		4, 5	7, 8	7, 8	8, 9	1
	Northern/Southern Hemispheres			7	7	8	1
	Eastern/Western Hemispheres			8	8	9	1
	Tropics of Capricorn/Cancer					8	7
	Arctic/Antarctic Circles					8	7

		LEVEL A	LEVEL B	LEVEL C	LEVEL D	LEVEL E	LEVEL F
Grids	Grid Coordinates/Map index			6	3	7	4
Graphs	Pictograph			9			
	Bar Graph			9	9	12	12
	Line Graph			9	9	12	12
	Circle Graph			9	9	12	12
	Time Line			9	9		
	Flow Chart			9	9		
	Tables					12	12
Landforms	Types of Landforms		1	4	6	5	5
	Landform Maps			4			
	Relief Maps				6	5	5
	Physical Maps/Elevation					5	5
Types of Maps	Route Maps			5	5	4	4
	Resource Maps			3	1		9
	Special Purpose Maps				1	6	8, 9
	Combining Maps/Comparing Maps						8, 9
	Historical Maps					6	
	Climate Maps						7, 8
	Land Use Maps						9
	Inset Maps		7			3	3
Time Zones	Time zones defined					11	10
	International Date Line						10
Temperature Zones	Low latitudes					10	7
	Middle latitudes					10	7
	High latitudes					10	7
	Sun/Earth relationship					10	7
Projections	Projections defined						11
	Mercator						11
	Robinson						11
	Polar						1, 11

Geography Themes

OBJECTIVES

Students will

◆ identify the five geographic themes: location, place, human/environment interaction, movement, and regions

◆ describe a location

◆ identify the physical and human features of a city

◆ give examples of how people interact with their environment

◆ give examples of the movement of people, goods, information, and ideas

◆ recognize a region and identify its common characteristics

VOCABULARY

geography	human features
themes	human/environment
location	interaction
place	movement
physical features	regions

INTRODUCING THE FIVE THEMES OF GEOGRAPHY

◆ In 1984 a joint committee of the National Council for Geographic Education and the Association of American Geographers published the *Guidelines for Geographic Education: Elementary and Secondary Schools*. This publication outlined the five fundamental themes in geography—location, place, human/environment interaction, movement, and regions. These themes help geographers and geography students organize the information they gather as they study Earth and its people.

◆ **Location** is the position of people and places on Earth. Location is described in two ways—absolute location and relative location. Absolute location is described using a specific address based on a grid system. Latitude and longitude make up the absolute location of a place based on the intersection of lines of latitude and lines of longitude. Relative location describes a location in relation to what it is near or what is around it. One example of using relative location is by giving directions. How would you tell a friend to get to your house from the local library? The special feature about location is on pages 76 and 77.

◆ **Place** is described by two kinds of features—physical features and human features. Physical features include such natural features as landforms, altitude, climate, soil, vegetation, and animal life. Human features are those created or developed by people. These can include roads, buildings, land use, population, religion, government, and other ways of life. The special feature about place is on pages 20 and 21.

◆ **Human/Environment Interaction** describes the relationships within places and the interaction of people and their environment—how people adapt to their environment. For example, people in areas with frequent hurricanes might use special building materials to withstand the effects of hurricanes. Another aspect of human/environment interaction is the way that people change their environment to meet their needs and wants. For example, a logging company cuts down trees to make lumber. The special feature about human/environment interaction is on pages 48 and 49.

◆ **Movement** describes the way people, goods, information, and ideas move from one part of Earth to another by way of transportation and communication. Movement is the study of the interdependence of people, the linkages between places, and the patterns of movement involving people, goods, information, and ideas. The special feature on movement is on pages 34 and 35.

◆ **Regions** are the basic units of geographic study. Regions are a way to organize information about areas with common features. Geographers use physical and human features as criteria to draw regional boundaries. Some physical features used include climate, landforms, natural resources, and vegetation. Some human features used include cultural beliefs, language, government, and economics. Regions can be as small as neighborhoods or as large as continents. The special feature about regions is on pages 62 and 63.

TEACHING NOTES

Pages 4-7   Read and discuss the activities with students. Point out to students that they will learn more about the five themes of geography in special features called "Geography Themes Up Close," found throughout *Maps•Globes•Graphs*.

EXTENSION ACTIVITIES

◆ As students study places in geography, have them organize the information by making charts using the five themes of geography as the headings. This will help students understand that the themes are organizational tools used in studying geography.

AT HOME ACTIVITY

◆ Divide the class into five groups—one group for each of the five themes. Ask students to use newspapers and magazines to find examples in pictures, advertisements, and stories that relate to their theme. Students can assemble their findings in a booklet or poster they can share with the class.

OBJECTIVES

Students will
◆ identify cardinal and intermediate directions
◆ locate north on a map, then use it to determine other directions
◆ determine relative location
◆ locate places on globes and maps

MATERIALS NEEDED

Transparencies 1, 2
compasses

VOCABULARY

North Pole · compass rose
South Pole · intermediate directions
cardinal directions

INTRODUCING THE SKILL

◆ Divide the class into groups. Show students how to use a compass to find north. Have students face north. Remind them that when they face north, south is behind them, east is to the right, and west is to the left. Have each group use masking tape to make a compass rose on the floor. Then have students direct each other around obstacles in the classroom by giving directions such as, "Take three steps west," and "Take two steps southeast."

◆ Give oral instructions for making simple geometric shapes, such as squares, rectangles, and triangles. Have students use their rulers and listen for cardinal and intermediate directions. For example, you might say, "Make an east-to-west line two inches long. From the west end of this line, draw a one-inch line going straight north. At the end of that line, draw another line going two inches to the east. At the end of this line, draw a one-inch line going south." Draw the correct figure (*a rectangle*) on the overhead projector as a check.

TEACHING NOTES

Page 8 Use Transparency 1 to introduce the concepts on this page.
Page 9 Use Transparency 2 to introduce the concepts on this page. Point out to students that cartographers, or mapmakers, use a compass rose to show directions. If the map doesn't have a compass rose, an arrow pointing north, or some other symbol to indicate direction, north should be at the top of the map.
Page 10 Have students use the map of the United States on page 94. Have them locate their state, then determine what borders their state in each cardinal direction. Then ask them, or have pairs of students ask each other, what direction other states are from their state.

Page 11 Explain to students that locator maps, like the inset map of the United States shown on this page, are used to help show the relationship of a place to a larger area.
Page 12 Provide students with more practice using directions on a map. Have students add and label the following within the park boundaries on the map on this page: Mt. Angeles (*south of Port Angeles and northeast of Hurricane Ridge*); Mt. Carrie (*southwest of Hurricane Ridge and northeast of Mt. Olympus*); Deer Park Campground (*in the northeast corner of the park and southeast of Hurricane Ridge*); Elwha Campground (*northwest of Hurricane Ridge and northeast of Sol Duc Hot Springs*).
Page 13 Have students label the states shown in green on this page. Then ask them to identify the locations of these states in relationship to the states shown in pink.

EXTENSION ACTIVITIES

◆ Divide the class into small groups to plan a hiking/camping trip through a national park. (Maps of national parks can be found in *The World Book Encyclopedia* and in the *Rand McNally Road Atlas* or from the U.S. Department of the Interior, National Park Service.) Have each group draw a map of a park, showing the boundaries and labeling points of interest. Their map should include a title, compass rose, legend, and the route for their trip. Then have them write a description of their trip, as if they had really taken it, using cardinal and intermediate directions.
◆ Have students work in pairs to make locator maps for the other maps in Chapter 1.
◆ Have students investigate and demonstrate different ways of finding north and determining direction if they have no compass, such as using the sun, the stars, aspects of nature, magnetized needles floating in water, and so on.
◆ Divide the class in half to create two teams. Hold a "geography bee" by having each team take turns naming a place, using a wall map of the world. Ask students, "What place is (give cardinal or intermediate direction) of (give reference point)?" Give one point for each correct answer. The winning team is the one that has the most points at the end of a time period that you specify.

AT HOME ACTIVITY

◆ Have students work with a family member to prepare directions for a treasure hunt. Have them hide a small "treasure" in their home or yard. Their directions for the treasure hunt should be written using cardinal and intermediate directions. Another family member or friend should read the directions to find the "treasure."

2 Symbols and Legends

OBJECTIVES

Students will
- use symbols and legends to read maps
- find the purpose of a map by reading the title
- find and recognize the symbols for capital cities, state boundaries, and international boundaries on political maps

MATERIALS NEEDED

Transparency 3
maps that show different kinds of political boundaries—counties, provinces, parishes, tax districts, school districts, townships, states, countries
Blackline Masters T26 and T28–T33

VOCABULARY

symbol	international boundary
legend	title
state boundary	political map

INTRODUCING THE SKILL

- Bring in maps that show different kinds of political boundaries—counties, provinces, parishes, tax districts, school districts, townships, states, countries, and so on. Discuss the various political entities and boundaries.
- Discuss with students how color is sometimes used on political maps to make divisions between states or countries easy to see. Have students find maps or globes that use color in this way.

TEACHING NOTES

Page 14 Use Transparency 3 to introduce the concepts on this page. Explain to students that bodies of water often form boundaries between states and countries. Ask students to name the bodies of water labeled on this map that make up state or international boundaries in the United States. (*Pacific Ocean, Atlantic Ocean, Arctic Ocean, Gulf of Mexico, Rio Grande, Mississippi River, Ohio River, Columbia River, Lake Superior, Lake Michigan, Lake Huron, Lake Ontario, Lake Erie*) Point out to students that sometimes mapmakers do not put boundary lines along bodies of water.

Page 15 Have students locate Mexico on a world map. Ask students questions about Mexico's location in relationship to other countries.

Page 16 Have students note that the north arrow on the compass rose does not point directly to the top of the map. Ask students why they think this is so. Then have them locate Central America on a wall map of the world or on the atlas map on pages 92–93. Ask: On what continent is Central America located? (*North America*) What continent is southeast of Central America? (*South America*) How do you think Central America got its name? (*It is between North America and South America.*)

Page 17 Ask students to name Canada's territories. (*Yukon Territory, the Northwest Territories and Nunavut.*) Ask students to estimate the amount of Canada's land area that these territories make up. (*more than one third*) Ask them to think of reasons why less than one percent of Canada's population live in these territories. (*remote location, severe climate, terrain is mostly forest-covered mountains and frozen wasteland*) Explain to students that Nunavut (which means "Our Land") is the home of the Inuit people. Nunavut became Canada's third territory on April 1, 1999.

Page 18 Have students locate the West Indies on a wall map of the world or a globe. Ask them to identify the countries located near the West Indies.

Page 19 Have students make a "map check" similar to the one on the bottom of this page for the map of the United States on page 14 or the map of Central America on page 16. Have students exchange and complete each other's "map checks."

EXTENSION ACTIVITIES

- Give students copies of the blackline map of North America on page T28. Have them use the maps in Chapter 2 to draw state boundaries in the United States and Mexico, and province and territory boundaries in Canada on the blackline map. Then have students add labels for the countries, states, provinces, and territories in North America. Have them color their map so that no bordering states or countries have the same color.
- Have students find out more about Nunavut, Canada's newest territory. Tell students that they can contact the Canadian government in Ottawa, Ontario, or if possible, visit the Nunavut website at www.nunavut.com.
- Give students copies of the **Map Attack!** blackline on page T26. Have students complete numbers 1–4 and 9 using classroom maps.
- Divide the class into small groups. Provide each group with a copy of a continent from the blackline masters on pages T28–T33. Have them make a political map of their continent.

AT HOME ACTIVITY

- Have students work with a family member to find political maps in newspapers and magazines. Have them discuss the purpose of each map and the symbols used to show boundaries.

Geography Themes Up Close

OBJECTIVES

Students will

◆ use map keys and symbols to locate and label places on maps

◆ describe and identify the physical features of places using maps

◆ describe the human features of places using maps

◆ compare the features of places

VOCABULARY

place

INTRODUCING THE SKILL

◆ Make sure students understand the distinction between physical features and human features. Explain that physical features are the natural features of a place that are part of the environment—climate, soil, landforms, bodies of water, and plants and animals. Human features are those created or developed by people that make up their culture, such as art and architecture, types of government, religions, ways of making a living, languages, and so on. Then, have students describe things in their town or city that makes it different from any other place.

◆ Have students brainstorm lists of things that make the United States different from Canada and Mexico. Students should indicate things such as landforms, climate, bodies of water, natural resources, language, customs, foods, governments, and populations. Call on volunteers to write their lists on the chalkboard for later use. Explain that in this feature, they will learn more about the things that make countries and other places different from one another.

TEACHING NOTES

Page 20   Read and discuss with students the introductory paragraph on page 20. Then ask students to classify the items on the lists of the things that make the United States different from Canada and Mexico as physical features or human features. Ask students if they can add any physical features or human features to the lists.

◆ Have students complete the activity on this page. Then call on volunteers to share their answers. Point out that the physical features and human features of Florida that they described in their answers make the state of Florida different from any other state. Ask students to describe how Florida is different from the states of Alaska, Connecticut, Minnesota, Oklahoma, and other states.

◆ Have students look at the map of Olympic National Park on page 12. Ask: What physical features of Olympic National Park make it unique? (*Lake Crescent, Sol Duc Hot Springs, Hurricane Ridge, Hoh Rain Forest, Mt. Olympus, Enchanted Valley*) What human features might you find in Olympic National Park? (*Roads, hiking trails, camp sites, refreshment stands, information center*)

Page 21   Have students answer the questions and work the exercise on this page.

◆ Next, ask students what physical features of Ottawa are not shown on the map. (*Answers may include climate, plant and animal life, and altitude.*) What human features might Ottawa have that are not shown on the map? (*Answers might include houses, streets, businesses, playgrounds, and bridges.*)

EXTENSION ACTIVITIES

◆ Point out to students that Ottawa, Ontario, and Mexico City, Mexico, are the national capitals of their countries. Provide students with travel brochures from Mexico City, Mexico. Ask students to use the brochures and the map of Ottawa in their text to compare and contrast the physical and human features of Mexico City with those of Ottawa. Have students organize their findings in Venn diagrams. Display the diagrams in the classroom.

◆ Assign students different national capitals in the world to research. Have them write reports about the national capitals describing the human and physical features. The report also should include a map showing some of the features of the national capitals. Have students share their reports with the class.

◆ Have students design their own travel brochures of North America.

AT HOME ACTIVITY

◆ Have students work with family members to create a map of physical and human features that make their neighborhood or town unique. Display the maps in the classroom.

OBJECTIVES

Students will
◆ use a map scale to determine distances on a map
◆ compare the scale on an inset map with the scale on a larger map

MATERIALS NEEDED

several United States maps in different sizes
Transparency 4
Blackline Masters T26 and T27
tape measures, yardsticks

VOCABULARY

map scale   kilometers
miles   inset map

INTRODUCING THE SKILL

◆ Make a map of the classroom using a grid on an overhead projector. First, have students measure the dimensions of the room in feet or yards. Then determine a scale for the map by having one square on the grid stand for a certain number of feet or yards so the map fits easily on the grid. Then show students how to draw the map to this scale. Have students tell where on the map you should add desks and other classroom items. Include the scale used on the map (for example: 1 square = 2 feet). Explain to students that cartographers, or mapmakers, use map scales to show how distance on a map compares with the distance in a real place.
◆ Divide the class into small groups. Distribute several maps of different sizes showing the United States. Have students compute how many miles one inch equals on each map scale. Record the findings in the form of a table on the chalkboard so students can compare the different map scales. Discuss with students that even though the map scales are different, the actual distance between two places is the same on all of the maps.

TEACHING NOTES

Page 22   Before teaching page 22, review how to convert fractional parts of an inch to decimal numbers. Then review multiplying whole numbers by decimal numbers. After teaching page 22, you may want to review an alternate way of measuring distances on a map. Show students how to mark the distance between two places on the edge of a piece of paper and compare that to the map scale.
Page 23   Use Transparency 4 to introduce the concepts on this page. Point out to students that distances computed using map scales are approximate. Have students use the steps shown on page 22 to find the distances between the following cities: Salem and Los Angeles (*770 miles*);

Detroit and Houston (*1,100 miles*); Dallas and Lincoln (*550 miles*); Houston and New York City (*1,430 miles*); Chattanooga and Houston (*660 miles*).
Page 24   Explain that these distances are not actual traveling distances by car or truck, since roads and highways are laid with respect to land features.
Page 25   Give students additional practice with figuring distances. Have them take a "flying trip" around the Great Lakes using the map on this page. Tell them that their plane will land in ten cities. They should start and end their trip in Thunder Bay. Have them draw a line from city to city and compute the distance between each city. Students should make a table of their findings. Finally, have students find the total distance of their trip.
Page 27   Provide students with copies of the **Map Attack!** blackline on page T26. Have students complete numbers 1–5 and 9 using maps from their social studies textbook or maps from newspapers and magazines.

EXTENSION ACTIVITIES

◆ Have students work with a partner to compute the approximate distances from Juneau, Alaska, and Honolulu, Hawaii, to Washington, D.C., using a world map.
◆ Divide the class into small groups. Assign each group a territory, possession, or commonwealth of the United States to research in encyclopedias and almanacs. Have them make travel brochures showing the following information: name of territory, possession, or commonwealth; year acquired; how acquired; land size; capital; population; approximate distance from their community to the capital of the territory, possession, or commonwealth; location relative to their state; and points of interest.
◆ Have students use a tape measure or a yardstick to determine the distance from their classroom door to the doorway of other places in the school building, such as the cafeteria, office, and gym. Then have students draw a map of the school, using symbols for the different places in the school. The map should include the following: map title, map scale, compass rose, and legend.
◆ Have students compute in kilometers the distances measured in this unit.

AT HOME ACTIVITY

◆ Provide students with copies of the United States map on page T27. Have them work with a family member to plan a vacation trip in the United States. They should draw their travel plans on the map, labeling at least five cities or points of interest they will visit. Have them calculate the round-trip distance in miles and kilometers.

OBJECTIVES

Students will
◆ read and interpret symbols on a route map
◆ distinguish between types of highways
◆ recognize regions of the United States
◆ recognize and use mileage markers

MATERIALS NEEDED

The Phantom Tollbooth by Norton Juster
Transparency 5
a route map of your state
a road atlas
Blackline Master T35
computerized simulation game *The Oregon Trail*

VOCABULARY

route	scenic road
interstate highway	region
U.S. highway	mileage marker
state highway	

INTRODUCING THE SKILL

◆ Read to students the first chapter of *The Phantom Tollbooth* by Norton Juster. Then have students draw a picture of the map that Milo received in a package. Their maps should include the following: ". . . principal roads, rivers and seas, towns and cities, mountains and valleys, intersections and detours, and sites of outstanding interest both beautiful and historic." Have students share their maps. Explain to students that in Chapter 4 they will learn how to read route maps.

◆ Give students opportunities to look at various route maps. Then ask them to brainstorm useful purposes of route maps. (*planning routes to take on a trip, finding the location of places, giving information about things to see and do, and estimating how long it will take to drive to a place*)

TEACHING NOTES

Page 28 Use Transparency 5 to introduce the concepts on this page. Divide the class into small groups. Give each group a copy of a route map of their state. Have students write questions about their state similar to those on this page. Have the groups exchange questions and answer them.

Page 29 Help students calculate the following problem: About how long would it take to get from Chicago to New York City if your car was traveling at a constant speed of 65 miles per hour? (*12.78 hours, or about 12 hours and 45 minutes*) Then have them make up and compute other story problems based on mileage amounts shown on the map.

Have students use road maps and atlases to locate the major highways in the states of Alaska and Hawaii. Then have students add these highways to the inset maps of Alaska and Hawaii on this page.

Page 30 Point out to students that in our highway system, east-west routes have even numbers, and north-south routes have odd numbers.

Page 31 Demonstrate how to read mileage charts in road atlases.

Page 32 Have students draw and label the following cities on the map: Decatur (*39 miles northeast of Springfield on I-72*); Effingham (*74 miles south of Champaign on I-57*); East St. Louis (*90 miles southwest of Springfield on I-55*); Indianapolis (*126 miles east of Champaign on I-74*). Students might check their approximate placement of the cities by referring to road maps of Illinois and Indiana.

Page 33 Have students name two interstate routes from Austin, Texas, to Santa Fe, New Mexico. (*Answers should include two of the following: I-35 north to I-40, I-40 west to I-25, I-25 northeast to Santa Fe; I-35 south to I-10, I-10 northwest to I-25, I-25 north and northeast to Santa Fe; I-35 north to I-20, I-20 west and southwest to I-10, I-10 northwest to I-25, I-25 north and northeast to Santa Fe.*)

EXTENSION ACTIVITIES

◆ Divide the class into seven groups. Assign a region of the United States to each group. Have students draw a map of their region, labeling major transportation centers (*railroad, airports, and seaports*) and routes (*highways, railroads, and inland waterways*). The maps should include a title, compass rose, legend, and map scale (if possible). On a bulletin board, assemble the maps in the form of a wall map of the United States.

◆ Ask students to name routes other than highways. (*railways, seaways, bicycle paths, airplane routes, cattle trails, horse trails, etc.*) Have students research and draw maps of routes other than highway routes.

◆ Divide the class into groups of five. Have them play the computerized simulation game *The Oregon Trail* to learn about the route that pioneers took to get from Independence, Missouri, to Oregon.

AT HOME ACTIVITY

◆ Have students tape-record an interview with older relatives, friends, or neighbors about U.S. Route 66. Have students ask: What do you know about U.S. Route 66? Why was this highway built? What states did it pass through? Have students share their interviews with the class.

Geography Themes Up Close

OBJECTIVES

Students will
- describe movement of people, goods, information, and ideas
- interpret a map of a major waterway
- analyze a chart about communication tools

MATERIALS NEEDED

Map of the St. Lawrence Seaway and the Mississippi River to the Gulf of Mexico
song "The Wreck of the Edmund Fitzgerald," by Gordon Lightfoot

VOCABULARY

movement
interdependence
charts

INTRODUCING THE SKILL

- Have students explain why human activities require movement. Ask them to name communication and transportation networks that they or their family members use daily, weekly, monthly, and yearly. For example, they may take the bus to school each day, take a train to a city once a week, drive in the family car to a relative's house once a month, or take a trip on an airplane once a year. They may read the daily newspaper, search the Internet once a week, read a magazine once a month, or send a fax once a year. Explain that in this feature, they will learn more about the geographic theme of movement.

TEACHING NOTES

Page 34   Read and discuss with students the introductory paragraph on page 34. Call on students to explain how interdependence may affect them and their friends and family members.
- Ask students to look at the map on page 34. Ask volunteers to point out the St. Lawrence River, the Great Lakes, the Illinois River, and the Mississippi River. Tell students that the St. Lawrence River and the seaway help make the ports on the Great Lakes some of the busiest ports in the world. Inform them that although the Atlantic Ocean and the Great Lakes have different elevations, a series of locks and canals (human features) enable ships to navigate the seaway. There are about 65 miles of canals, 15 locks, and 3 dams along the St. Lawrence Seaway. If possible, show pictures of the locks and canals or point them out on a map. Tell students that the United States and Canada began construction on the seaway in 1954 and completed it in 1959. This seaway plays an important role in the economies of both nations: the St. Lawrence Seaway handles about 50 million short tons (45 million metric tons) of cargo each year. About 40 percent of this cargo moves between North America and countries overseas.
- Play the song "The Wreck of the Edmund Fitzgerald," by Gordon Lightfoot for students. This song tells about the loss of the Great Lakes ore freighter, the *S.S. Edmund Fitzgerald*, in a storm on Lake Superior in 1975.
- Discuss with students the importance of a waterway network like the one shown the map, in comparison to other transportation networks such as highways and railways for transporting people and goods. (*Shipping goods on waterways is generally less expensive than shipping by truck, rail, or air. This waterway system gives people in the United States and Canada a convenient and relatively inexpensive way to move goods to large portions of both countries.*) Show students on a map how the St. Lawrence Seaway connects to the Mississippi River (via the Illinois River) and then on to the Gulf of Mexico.

Page 35   Ask students the following questions about the chart: If you wanted to advertise a product, which communication tool would you use to reach the largest number of people? Do people spend more time getting information from books or magazines? How does the information on television differ from information in newspapers?

EXTENSION ACTIVITIES

- Have students find more information on the St. Lawrence Seaway: the locks and canals, the kinds of ships that operate on the seaway, the kinds of cargo hauled, where goods are shipped to and from, and so on. Ask students to report their findings, using illustrations, posters, models, dioramas, etc.
- If possible, help students search the Internet for copies of newspapers from other states or from Mexico and Canada. If possible, ask them to print the newspapers. Allow students time to review the newspapers to compare and contrast the newspaper styles.
- Ask students to hypothesize about transportation and communication in the future. How might it be different than it is today? Have them share their ideas with the class.

AT HOME ACTIVITY

- Have students work with family members to collect labels of goods from other states and Mexico and Canada. Then display the labels around the borders of a large world map on the bulletin board. Use yarn or ribbons to connect each label to its country of origin. Take time to have students describe and explain their labels to the class.

OBJECTIVES

Students will
- identify and compare features on a physical map
- use symbols to determine elevation on a physical map
- distinguish between relief and elevation

MATERIALS NEEDED

A map showing the route of Lewis and Clark's expedition
Blackline Masters T27 and T35
Transparency 6
The Way to the Western Sea: Lewis and Clark Across the Continent by David Lavender or *This Vast Land: A Young Man's Journal of the Lewis and Clark Expedition* by Stephen E. Ambrose

VOCABULARY

relief map	sea level
mountain range	elevation
plain	physical map

INTRODUCING THE SKILL

- Explain to students that President Thomas Jefferson commissioned Meriwether Lewis and William Clark to explore the Louisiana Territory after it was purchased from France in 1803. Lewis and Clark kept detailed journals describing the lands through which they traveled. Show students the route of Lewis and Clark's expedition from St. Louis, Missouri, to the Pacific Ocean. (You can find a copy of their route in history texts and *The World Book Encyclopedia*.) Ask students to name the landforms that Lewis and Clark explored. (*Missouri River, Great Plains, Rocky Mountains, Columbia River*) Next, read students an excerpt from *The Way to the Western Sea: Lewis and Clark Across the Continent* by David Lavender (Harper Collins) or from *This Vast Land: A Young Man's Journal of the Lewis and Clark Expedition* by Stephen E. Ambrose (Simon & Schuster Children's Publishing). Discuss the descriptions of the landforms Lewis and Clark explored.
- Divide the class into small groups. Provide students with copies of the blackline map of the United States on page T27. Have students use encyclopedias, almanacs, geography books, and atlases, on a "Largest Landform Hunt." Ask them to find the country's highest mountain (*Mount McKinley in Alaska*), longest river (*Missouri River*), biggest desert (*Death Valley in California*), and largest lake (*Lake Superior*). Have students draw and label those features on their map. Tell them that in Chapter 5 they will learn to identify landforms on physical maps.

TEACHING NOTES

Page 36 Use Transparency 6 to introduce the concepts on this page.

Page 37 Have students compare the physical map of the United States on this page with the atlas map of the United States on page 94. Have students identify the landforms and elevations in individual states and capital cities.

Page 38 Ask students to make generalizations about land use in the Mountain and Pacific states based on elevation and on the location of landforms. Then compare their generalizations with land-use maps of these regions, found in encyclopedias, geography books, and atlases.

Page 39 Ask students to compare the landforms and elevations in the Mountain and Pacific states with the landforms and elevations in the Northeast.

Page 40 Have students draw where major highways would be located in Washington, based on the locations of landforms. Have students compare their map with a Washington route map.

Page 41 Explain to students that, in general, the greater the elevation, the cooler the climate will be. Have them study the physical maps on pages 40 and 41 and make generalizations about the climate in Washington and in Pennsylvania.

EXTENSION ACTIVITIES

- Provide students with copies of the blackline world map on page T35. Have students work in pairs to play "Largest Landform Hunt" and find and label the largest landforms for each continent.
- Divide the class into seven groups. Assign a region of the United States to each group. Have students make a relief map of their assigned region, showing state boundaries and landforms and labeling the states and landforms.
- Provide students with copies of the blackline world map on page T35. Have them make relief maps of the world.
- Have students read *Down the Colorado* by Eliot Porter with John Wesley Powell. This book contains the diary written by American geologist John Wesley Powell in 1869 on his first boat trip through the Grand Canyon on the Colorado River. Have students draw pictures using Powell's descriptions of the landforms in the canyon.

AT HOME ACTIVITY

- Have students work with a family member to make a profile of the United States, like the one shown on page 37, out of a dough mixture. The dough can be made by mixing the following ingredients: 2 cups flour, $\frac{1}{2}$ cup salt, 2 teaspoons cream of tartar, 1 cup water, and food coloring.

OBJECTIVES

Students will

◆ use titles and legends to read and interpret a variety of special purpose maps, including precipitation, temperature, historical, population, land use, and resource maps

MATERIALS NEEDED

Transparency 7
Blackline Masters T26, T27, T28

VOCABULARY

special purpose map
symbol
resource map

population map
temperature map

INTRODUCING THE SKILL

◆ Have students pretend they are going on vacation in Africa. Ask them what kinds of information they would want to know about Africa before they went there. Write their responses on the chalkboard. (*Responses might include: climate, distance from their community, interesting places to visit, languages spoken in each country, transportation routes, etc.*) Point out that these are all things they can learn from maps. Explain to students that in Chapter 6 they will learn about special purpose maps.

◆ Ask students to bring newspapers and current-events magazines to school. Then give students ten minutes to find a map in a magazine or a newspaper. Have students discuss the different kinds of maps that they found. Explain that a map that gives a particular kind of information is called a special purpose map. Ask students how they might categorize the maps. (*Examples: climate maps, resource maps, historical maps, etc.*) Display the maps on a bulletin board.

TEACHING NOTES

Page 42 Use Transparency 7 to introduce the concepts on this page. Then, have students brainstorm a list of uses for precipitation maps.

Page 43 Point out to students that geographers study many special purpose maps to form generalizations about places. Have students study the maps on pages 42 and 43 and then make generalizations about the climate of the United States.

Page 44 Have students use their map attack skills to read historical maps in their social studies textbook or in encyclopedias.

Page 45 Have students compare this map with the relief map of the United States on page 36. Ask students: Which landforms have the most people living there? Which landforms have the fewest people living there? What other special purpose maps might help explain the population patterns in the United States? (*climate, resource, transportation, etc.*)

Page 46 Ask students the following questions about the map on this page: Which Southwest state produces the most oil? (*Texas*) In which state is copper the most plentiful mineral? (*Arizona*) In which Southwest states is gold found? (*southeastern Arizona and western New Mexico*) In what part of Oklahoma are beef cattle raised? (*northern*)

EXTENSION ACTIVITIES

◆ Give students copies of the blackline map of North America on page T28. Have students work in pairs to research explorers, such as Sir Francis Drake, Sir Walter Raleigh, La Salle, Cabeza de Vaca, Balboa, and Pizarro. Ask students to draw and label the routes of the explorers they researched. Have them make a legend similar to the one on page 36.

◆ Collect several weather maps from newspapers. Divide the class into small groups. Give each group a weather map. Have students in each group make up several questions about the weather map. Then have groups exchange and answer the questions.

◆ Have students choose a state and make an atlas of four or five special purpose maps for that state. Remind them to include a title and a legend for each map. Ask them to design a cover for the atlas.

◆ Provide students with copies of the blackline map of the United States on page T27. Have students research and make a map showing the Wheat Belt and the Cotton Belt of the United States. Then have students compare their map with the precipitation map on page 42. Have them make generalizations about the amount of precipitation needed to produce these crops.

AT HOME ACTIVITY

◆ Give students copies of the **Map Attack!** blackline on page T26. Have students work with a family member to find an example of a special purpose map in a newspaper or a magazine and complete the **Map Attack!**, numbers 1–5 and 9.

Geography Themes Up Close

OBJECTIVES

Students will
- interpret maps showing the impact of human/environment interaction on the environment
- interpret a resource map
- identify and explain the economic activities in areas

VOCABULARY

human/environment interaction
acid rain

INTRODUCING THE SKILL

- Ask students to list ways that people depend on the environment and ways people change the environment. Call on volunteers to share their lists with the class. Explain to the class that in this feature they will examine instances of the interaction of humans and the environment.

TEACHING NOTES

Page 48 Read and discuss the introductory paragraph on page 48 with students.
- Discuss with students the impact of acid rain on parts of the United States and Canada. Ask: How does acid rain affect the environment? (*It kills fish and destroys forests*) How does acid rain affect the people who live in areas where the levels are high? (*The people are left with fewer fish and forests. Therefore people are losing their ways of life.*) What can be done to help stop acid rain? (*Burn less gas, coal, and oil.*)
Page 49 Have students read the paragraph and then use the map to answers the questions on this page. Discuss answers with students, especially the answers to the last question. Point out to students that people everywhere depend on the environment and its resources to meet their needs. The kinds of resources a place has help decide how people there will make their living.
- Ask students to compare and contrast the map of Land Use in the Plains States on page 46 with the map of Land Use and Resources in Mexico. Ask: How is land use in these two places similar? (*Both places use the land for farming and for manufacturing. Both places grow corn.*) How is land use in these two places different? (*Different crops are grown in the two places—Plains states grow barley, hay, and wheat. Mexico grows sugarcane, bananas, coffee, and cotton.*)

- Have students work in small groups to compare the physical map of the United States on page 36 and the population map of the United States on page 45. Ask them to write a generalization about the physical features of the United States and the population distribution of the United States. Have each group repeat this activity using the map of temperatures in the United States on page 43 and the population map of the United States on page 45. Have each group read their generalizations to the class.

EXTENSION ACTIVITIES

- Have students find pictures in newspapers and magazines of ways that people adapt to the environment. Create a bulletin board using the pictures.
- Have students research, using magazine articles, newspaper articles, and the Internet to examine the impact of acid rain on other countries of the world, especially Mexico. If possible, have students make maps showing the location and levels of acid rain in the world today. Also, have students write brief reports explaining the human/environment interactions that have led to increased levels of acid rain.
- Have students research the changes that have occurred in their local environment as a result of human or environment interaction. Then, have students create a scrapbook of pictures and drawings that illustrate the changes in their local environment over time. Students might find such information at their local library, town or city government building, local newspaper, or local historical museum.

AT HOME ACTIVITY

- Have students work with neighbors and family members to analyze changes in their neighborhood over time. Ask them to interview people who have lived in the neighborhood for many years. Have students prepare questions ahead of time for their interviews. Tell them to think of questions that require more than a one-word answer. Ask students to record the responses on paper. Some students may wish to videotape or tape-record their interview. Call on volunteers to share their interviews with the class. Have students list the changes that have occurred because of human interaction.

OBJECTIVES

Students will
◆ use a map index and grid coordinates to locate specific places on a map
◆ use a grid to determine relative direction

MATERIALS NEEDED

graph paper
Transparency 8
game markers (e.g., jelly beans)
Blackline Masters T26, T27, T28

VOCABULARY

grid
map index

INTRODUCING THE SKILL

◆ Provide students with graph paper. Have them make a grid of six squares by six squares. Ask them to label the columns of squares with the numbers 1 through 6 at the top and bottom of the grid. Then ask them to label the rows of squares with the letters A through F at each side of the grid. Tell students to draw connected lines from squares A-1 to D-6; D-6 to D-1; D-1 to A-6; A-6 to F-4; F-4 to A-1 to form a picture. (*star*) Then have students make up similar directions to form other pictures on a grid. Have students give their directions to a partner. Explain to students that in Chapter 7 they will learn about locating places using map grids.

TEACHING NOTES

Page 50   Use Transparency 8 to introduce the concepts on this page. Then, have students add and label the following landmarks on the map: Washington Square (*the green square southwest of Independence Hall*); Betsy Ross House (*southwest of the Benjamin Franklin Bridge, northeast of Independence Hall, between 2nd and 4th streets*); Tourist Information Center (*northwest of City Hall, south of Cherry Street, east of 16th Street*). Ask students to name the grid square where each landmark is located (*Washington Square D-4; Betsy Ross House C-5; Tourist Information Center C-3*).

Page 51   After students have completed this page, have them make an index for the map on page 50.

Page 52   Point out the location of Washington, D.C., on a wall map of the United States. Have students name the states that border it. Explain to students that Washington, D.C., was one of the few cities in the country that was designed before it was built.

Page 53   Have students research and add points of interest to the map of New York City and the map index. Detailed maps of cities can be found in

Rand McNally Road Atlas and in *The World Book Encyclopedia.*

Page 54   Have students locate Lombard Street at the top of the map. Ask students if they know what the squiggle on Lombard Street means. Then explain that this street in San Francisco is known as The Crookedest Street in the World because it makes eight sharp turns in a single block.

Page 55   After students have completed page 55, have them form groups of three or four to play "Map Bingo." Give students markers, such as popcorn or jelly beans. One student is the "caller" and asks location questions about the map on page 55, such as "Where is City Hall?" Other students should scan the index, find the correct grid square, and put their marker where the building appears on the map. After asking four location questions, the "caller" should check the other students' answers by calling the correct grid squares for each question. Those who have the correct grid squares covered may eat their markers. Choose new "callers," and repeat the game using the other maps in Chapter 7.

EXTENSION ACTIVITIES

◆ Have students work in pairs to plot a walking tour of Washington, D.C., using the map on page 52. Explain that their time is limited, so they can only visit seven points of interest. Tell students to write out directions for their tour, using the names of the points of interest and the cardinal and intermediate directions they would travel to get from place to place.

◆ Provide students with copies of the blackline maps on pages T27 or T28. Have them add a grid to their map, then add countries or states, cities, and points of interest. The map should include a title, compass rose, and map index.

◆ Provide students with copies of the **Map Attack!** blackline on page T26. Ask students to complete this using a map from Chapter 7.

◆ Divide the class into small groups. Provide each group with a city map. Have students use the index and grid to locate specific streets, parks, etc. Have students circle the locations on the maps. Then have them draw a route between two places and list the coordinates of the grids that the route passes through.

AT HOME ACTIVITY

◆ Show students that their phone book includes a map of their community with a map index. Have students work with a family member to practice finding specific places in their community using the phone book map.

OBJECTIVES

Students will
◆ recognize special lines of latitude
◆ recognize and use latitude coordinates
◆ locate the Northern and Southern Hemispheres

MATERIALS NEEDED

orange, permanent marker, knife
Transparency 9
Blackline Master T35

VOCABULARY

Equator	parallels
Northern Hemisphere	Tropic of Cancer
Southern Hemisphere	Tropic of Capricorn
hemisphere	Arctic Circle
latitude	Antarctic Circle
degrees	

INTRODUCING THE SKILL

◆ Compare the beginning sound of the word
latitude with the word *ladder*. The lines of latitude
are like the rungs of a ladder leading up or down a
map or globe. (Or use the rhyme "lat," for latitude
and "flat.")
◆ Demonstrate the fact that latitude lines run
parallel to one another and that they form circles.
Draw a line around the middle of an orange. Then
draw lines, similar to lines of latitude on a globe,
above and below the middle line. Next, cut the
orange along the middle line. Show students that
the orange has been cut in half. Next, cut the orange
halves along the other lines. Show students that
these cuts form circles. Ask students to describe the
sizes of these circles. (*They are decreasing in size from
the middle line.*) Also point out to students that the
lines never touch. Explain to students that if they
could cut a globe along its lines of latitude, the
circles would look similar to those on the orange.

TEACHING NOTES

Page 56   Use Transparency 9 to introduce the
concepts on this page. Point out that globes and
world maps generally show lines of latitude every
15 or 20 degrees. Explain that each line of latitude
forms a circle that runs in the same direction as the
Equator and parallel to the Equator.
Pages 57   Explain to students that the Tropic of
Cancer marks the northernmost places on Earth
where the sun shines directly overhead. The Tropic
of Capricorn marks the southernmost places on
Earth where the sun shines directly overhead. The
Arctic Circle and the Antarctic Circle mark the
edges of areas where the sun stays above the
horizon one or more nights during the year.

Page 58   Demonstrate the importance of
identifying lines of latitude as being either north or
south of the Equator. Ask students to name the
city located near 23$\frac{1}{2}$° (*Havana and São Paulo*).
Then ask them to name the city located near 23$\frac{1}{2}$°N
(*Havana*). Ask students to give the approximate
latitude of the other cities shown on this map.
Page 59   Ask students to name the hemisphere in
which each city is located.
Page 60   On a classroom map of North America
point out the long border between the United
States and Canada. Explain that the straight line of
the border across much of the West is set at the
49th parallel. Have students discuss the climate
and landforms along the 49th parallel. What do
they think it would be like to live at the border?

EXTENSION ACTIVITIES

◆ Discuss with students that lines of latitude can
be drawn at many different increments. Have them
find maps and compare the increments shown. Ask
questions to help students form conclusions, such
as "What kinds of maps show small increments?
What kinds of maps show larger increments?"
◆ Divide the class into small groups. Provide each
group with the following supplies: a globe, a
yardstick, and a piece of string about three feet
long. Have students measure the circumference
of the lines of latitude using the string and the
yardstick. Next, have them measure the distances
of these lines of latitude from the Equator. Have
each group record their findings in a table. Then,
have each group draw generalizations about their
findings. Discuss the generalizations as a class.
◆ Have students use encyclopedias and history
books to do research about the historical
significance of the following lines of latitude:
James Polk's slogan "Fifty-four Forty or Fight!";
the Missouri Compromise line of 36°30'; and the
38th parallel during the Korean War. Have
students write a report about their findings.
◆ Provide students with copies of the blackline
map of the world on page T35. Have students label
the continents, Equator, Tropic of Cancer, Tropic of
Capricorn, Arctic Circle, and Antarctic Circle. Then
have them list the continents and the degrees of
latitude that the continents lie between. They can
refer to the maps on pages 57 and 92–93 for help.

AT HOME ACTIVITIES

◆ Have students work with a family member to
plan a trip from their home to a place located on
the same line of latitude. Have them describe
where they would go, how many miles they would
travel to get there, and what they would do there.

Geography Themes Up Close

OBJECTIVES

Students will
- recognize the physical and human features that define regions
- draw inferences from maps showing regions
- distinguish ways that neighborhoods are different
- determine the criteria used to draw regional boundaries
- define a region as an area that has one or more common characteristics

MATERIALS NEEDED

Blackline Master T28

VOCABULARY

regions

INTRODUCING THE SKILL

◆ Have students identify special areas or districts in their community, such as a business district, shopping district, or school district. Ask: Why do communities have special areas? Explain that in this feature they will learn more about how places and areas can be designated as regions.

TEACHING NOTES

Page 62 Read and discuss with students the introductory paragraphs on page 62. Inform students that another name for an urban center is *megalopolis*. Explain that *megalopolis* is a Greek word that combines the Greek words *mega*, meaning "large," and *polis*, meaning "city." Therefore a *megalopolis* is a "large city." Tell students that each megalopolis is a region made up of two or more large cities and their suburbs and that a central city usually has a population of at least 50,000.

◆ Have students look at the map on this page. Ask: Do you live in an urban center? What is the common feature of the regions shown on this map? (*Population and size of cities that are close together*) What cities make up the Gulf Coast urban center? (*New Orleans and Houston*) What cities make up the Coastal Florida urban center? (*Jacksonville, Tampa, Miami*) Why are there no urban centers in the Plains states? (*There are few large cities and smaller populations there.*)

◆ Have interested students find out more about one of the urban centers shown on the map, such as population numbers, land size, etc. Then have students research cities in ancient Greece. Have students compare an urban center with an ancient Greek city, or *polis*.

◆ Ask students to find out more about the urban center regions that have developed outside the United States in the following countries: Japan (Tokyo-Yokohama-Osaka), Germany (the Ruhr Industrial Basin), the Netherlands, and Belgium. Ask students to report their findings in charts, posters, and/or maps.

◆ Ask students to find maps in atlases that show regions based on physical and human features. Have students work in small groups to determine the criteria used to draw the regional boundaries on the maps.

Page 63 Have students share their answers to questions 5–7 on this page. Discuss the answers to the last question and accept any reasonable response.

◆ Ask students to look at the map on page 50. Point out that this map shows part of Philadelphia called Chinatown. Point out that this is a region in Philadelphia where people of Chinese heritage live. This area has Chinese restaurants, shops that sell goods from China, and signs written in Chinese. Ask: Is this a physical or human region? Why?(*human, because it is based on human features—Chinese culture, language, etc.*)

◆ Have students look at the map of Boston on page 55. Point out that the region colored green along Boylston Street and Tremont Street is called Boston Common. Have them research to find out about the special features of this region.

EXTENSION ACTIVITIES

◆ Have students find other thematic maps in *Maps•Globes•Graphs*. Ask them to analyze the maps to determine the criteria on which each map is based.

◆ Have students compare political maps of North America in the 1700s with political maps of the same area today. Point out that regions change. Ask them what caused these political regions to change.

AT HOME ACTIVITY

◆ Provide students with copies of the outline map of North America on page T28. Have students work with family members to research and show regions of the United States on the map. They may use either a physical feature or a human feature as the criteria of their map.

OBJECTIVES

Students will

◆ locate lines of longitude on a globe or map, including the Prime Meridian
◆ locate the Eastern and Western Hemispheres
◆ recognize and use longitude coordinates
◆ locate places on a map using lines of latitude and longitude

MATERIALS NEEDED

Transparency 10
Blackline Master T34

VOCABULARY

Prime Meridian　　　Eastern Hemisphere
longitude　　　　　　Western Hemisphere
meridians

INTRODUCING THE SKILL

◆ Have students say *longitude* and think of the vertical, long lines on a map or globe. Ask students to find the imaginary lines on a globe that run from the North Pole to the South Pole. Show students a pumpkin or a peeled orange. Compare the curved lines with the lines of longitude on a globe.

◆ In order to demonstrate the importance of describing the location of a place by using lines of latitude and longitude, discuss with students the confusion that develops when two or more students in a class have the same first name. Brainstorm some solutions to this problem.

TEACHING NOTES

Page 64　Use Transparency 10 to introduce the concepts on this page. Divide the class into small groups. Provide each group with a globe. Have students trace the Prime Meridian (0° longitude) on the globe past the North or the South Pole to the other side of the globe. Have them note that the Prime Meridian and the 180° meridian form a circle that divides the globe in half. Then have them find and trace the 90°W meridian past the North or South Pole. Ask students. "What meridian forms a circle around the globe along with the 90°W meridian?" (*90°E meridian*) Have them trace other lines of longitude around the globe and list the pairs of lines that form a circle. Ask them to make a generalization. (*The sum is always 180°.*)

Page 65　Review with students the importance of labeling lines of longitude with E or W. Ask the following questions: Where is the 30° line of longitude? (*Students should respond that there is a line of longitude for 30°E and one for 30°W.*) What two lines of longitude are not labeled E or W? (*the Prime Meridian and the 180° meridian*) Why is this

so? (*because these lines of longitude divide the globe into the Eastern and Western Hemispheres*)

Page 66　Ask students why globes and world maps generally do not show all 360 lines of longitude. (*It would be too cluttered.*) Have students look at several world maps and at a globe. Have them identify the increments that have been used for the lines of longitude on the maps and globe. Then refer students to the map on this page. Point out that the lines of longitude have been drawn every 10° but that they are labeled only every 20°. Have students write labels for the unlabeled lines of longitude.

Page 67　Explain to students that in order to know the exact location of a place on Earth, you need to know its latitude and longitude. Dramatize this fact by saying, "I am thinking of a city that is located at 60°N. What city am I thinking of?" (*Anchorage, St. Petersburg, or Magadan*) Then say, "I am thinking of a city near the point where 60°N and 150°W cross. What city am I thinking of?" (*Anchorage*) Ask students to estimate the location of Santa Fe, Cairo, New Orleans, Brisbane, and Shanghai by using lines of latitude and longitude.

EXTENSION ACTIVITIES

◆ Refer students to the atlas map of the world on pages 92 and 93. Ask students, "Between which two lines of latitude shown is the Mississippi River?" (*20°N and 60°N*) Then ask, "Between which two lines of longitude shown is the Mississippi River?" (*80°W and 100°W*) Have students make a list of the rivers on the map and the lines of latitude and longitude they lie between.

◆ Refer students to the atlas map of the United States on page 94. Ask students to name the state capitals that are north of 45°N and west of 100°W. (*Bismarck, Helena, Olympia*) Then have students name the state capitals in the following areas: north of 30°N and between 95°W and 100°W (*Austin, Oklahoma City, Topeka, Lincoln*); south of 45°N and east of 70°W (*Augusta*); between 30°N and 40°N and between 115°W and 125°W (*Sacramento, Carson City*).

◆ Have students do research to find out why the Prime Meridian is located in Greenwich, England.

◆ Provide students with copies of the blackline map of the Eastern and Western Hemispheres on page T34. Have students work in pairs to label the lines of latitude and longitude in each hemisphere.

AT HOME ACTIVITY

◆ Have students play the game, "I am thinking of (a city, a landmark, or a landform) at (latitude and longitude)," with a family member. They might use the atlas on pages 92–93, other atlases, or a globe.

OBJECTIVES

Students will
- identify Earth's rotation as the cause of night and day
- identify areas of the world as being in the high latitudes, middle latitudes, or low latitudes.
- draw conclusions about a place's climate based on its location

MATERIALS NEEDED

globe and flashlight
Transparency 11
Blackline Masters T28, T34, T35

VOCABULARY

axis	low latitudes
rotation	high latitudes
climate zones	middle latitudes
climate	

INTRODUCING THE SKILL

- Show how day and night occur by using a globe and a flashlight. Tell students that the flashlight represents the sun and that Earth rotates counterclockwise. Rotate the globe, demonstrating why the East Coast gets sunlight before the rest of the United States. Put your finger on your state and ask students what time of day it is as you continue rotating the globe.

TEACHING NOTES

Page 70 Use Transparency 11 to introduce the concepts on this page. After teaching page 70, discuss with students that Earth revolves around the sun, as well as rotates on its axis. Demonstrate how the tilt of Earth causes the seasons. Have a student stand still to represent the sun. Hold a globe at a tilt, and ask which hemisphere (*northern or southern*) is nearest the "sun." What season would it be in that hemisphere? Move the globe 180° around the "sun," maintaining the same tilt. Now ask what season it would be. Ask how our weather would differ if Earth did not tilt. (*Each place on Earth would have the same climate year-round.*)

Page 71 Provide students with copies of the blackline map of the world on page T35. Have students label the continents and oceans. Then have them color the three climate zones in the following manner: low latitudes—red, middle latitudes—orange, high latitudes—yellow. Have them make a table showing which continents and oceans are located in each climate zone.

Page 72 Provide students with copies of the blackline maps of the Eastern and Western Hemispheres on page T34. Have students use the profile of the Eastern Hemisphere to make a diagram showing the climate zones, similar to the diagram shown on this page.

Page 73 Ask students the following questions: The United States is mostly in which climate zone? (*middle latitudes*) What state is partly in the high latitudes? (*Alaska*) What state is in the low latitudes? (*Hawaii*) Do you think the climate would be warmer in Washington, D.C., or in Juneau, Alaska? Why? (*Washington, D.C., would be warmer because it is closer to the low latitudes.*)

Page 74 Have students draw conclusions about the amount of rainfall a place receives, based on its latitude. (*Places in low latitudes generally receive more rainfall than places in middle and high latitudes. Places in middle latitudes receive more rainfall than places in high latitudes.*)

EXTENSION ACTIVITIES

- Tell students that the sun's effect upon Earth is only one part of what causes climate differences. Ask them to research some of the other factors that affect climate: wind, ocean currents, the water cycle, nearness to large bodies of water, and elevation. Have students present their findings by making a diagram or a flow chart or by role playing a meteorologist's report on television.
- Provide students with copies of the blackline map of North America on page T28. Have them use an atlas map to label each country. Then have them make a rainfall map of North America using the map on page 74 as reference. Discuss which countries receive the most rainfall and which receive the least.
- Have students work in small groups to research how Earth's movement around the sun causes seasons. Have half the groups make diagrams showing seasons in the Northern Hemisphere and the other groups make diagrams showing seasons in the Southern Hemisphere. Diagrams of seasons can be found in geography books and reference books about seasons or climate.
- Have students research and explain the terms *equinox* and *solstice*.

AT HOME ACTIVITY

- Have students work with a family member to keep a record of the time the sun rises and the time the sun sets each day for one week. They can estimate the times from their own observations, by listening to television weather reports, or by reading newspaper weather reports. Then, in class, have them discuss whether the days are getting shorter or longer and how this affects their lifestyle.

Geography Themes Up Close

OBJECTIVES

Students will
◆ locate places relative to other places and to physical features on maps
◆ use latitude and longitude to identify the absolute location of places in North America
◆ label locations of selected places on a map
◆ speculate on reasons for the locations of cities

VOCABULARY

location
relative location
absolute location

INTRODUCING THE SKILL

◆ Ask students to write down a description of the location of their home relative to the school. Call on volunteers to read their descriptions. Discuss with students the kinds of words used to describe the locations.
◆ On a wall map of the world, have students identify North America relative to other continents and the oceans. Explain to students that they will learn more about locations in this feature.

TEACHING NOTES

Page 76   Have students read the introductory paragraph on this page. Ask students to give examples of times when they would need to know the absolute location of a place. Ask students to give examples of situations in which they would need to know the relative location of a place.
◆ Have students look at the pictures of globes on page 8 of their textbooks. Ask students: In which hemispheres is North America located? (*Western Hemisphere and the Northern Hemisphere*) How would you describe the location of North America relative to the Equator? (*It is north of the Equator.*)
◆ Ask students to look at the map of the world on pages 92 and 93 in the Atlas of their textbook. What is the location of North America relative to the other continents? (*North America is north of South America, northwest of Africa, west of Europe, north of Antarctica, northwest of Australia, and west of Asia.*)
◆ Call on students to share their answers to question 4 on this page. Remind students that there are many ways of describing the relative location of a place.

Page 77   Ask for volunteers to share their answers to questions 5–7 on this page. Again, remind students that there are many ways of describing the relative location of a place. Also, explain that the absolute location of a landform is usually given as the latitude and longitude coordinates near the center or middle of the landform. Ask them to determine the absolute location of the Rocky Mountains. Have a student look in an atlas to see if the class was correct. You may need to show students where this kind of information is found in an atlas. Have students choose other landforms to determine their absolute locations.

EXTENSION ACTIVITIES

◆ Have students research to find out about the advantages and disadvantages to Hawaii's location relative to the United States. Ask students to write brief paragraphs explaining these advantages and disadvantages.
◆ Have students use globes to locate North America relative to other continents and the oceans. Ask students to explain how using a globe is different from using a map when finding relative and absolute locations.
◆ Have students make up relative-location riddles. An example riddle might be: I am a continent located north of Antarctica and south of Europe. Who am I? (*Africa*) The riddles should include landforms, bodies of water, countries, states, provinces, and cities. Be sure that all those participating in the game have access to maps of the world or globes.
◆ Encourage students to use the maps in local phone books to find the locations of their friends' homes and their favorite places to shop.

AT HOME ACTIVITY

◆ Have students work with family members to determine the relative and absolute location of the city or town in which they live. Then have students and family members write directions from their house to house of a friend or relative who lives at least a few miles away.

OBJECTIVES

Students will

◆ explain why time zones exist

◆ name the four time zones in the continental United States

◆ determine the time in a specific place, given the time in another time zone

MATERIALS NEEDED

Transparency 12

Blackline Masters T27, T28

VOCABULARY

time zones

INTRODUCING THE SKILL

◆ Review A.M. and P.M. with students. Tell them the following mnemonic devices: A.M. is "After Midnight" and P.M. is "Preparing for Midnight."

◆ Ask students when they might need to figure out the time in another time zone. (*traveling, watching TV programs, making long-distance phone calls, watching space launchings, etc.*)

TEACHING NOTES

Page 78 Use Transparency 12 to introduce the concepts on this page. Explain to students that time zones are about 1,000 miles across from east to west at the Equator. Ask students to determine the approximate circumference of Earth at the Equator after telling them that there are 24 time zones. (*1,000 miles x 24 = 24,000 miles*) Next, ask students about how many degrees wide each time zone is, if there are 24 time zones in 360 degrees. (*360 degrees ÷ 24 = 15 degrees*) Point out to students that although time zones are based on lines of longitude 15 degrees apart, time zones do not always follow along lines of longitude. Ask students to give reasons why they think this is so. (*state or national borders, landforms*)

Page 79 Ask students if they have ever noticed time changes discussed on TV. The major networks may advertise that a new show will be coming on at 7:30 P.M. Eastern Standard Time. Ask students to tell what time that would be in other time zones.

Page 80 Have students note the present time in their state or community. Then ask them what time it is in various other states. Ask students to debate the pros and cons of having all the United States in the same time zone.

Page 81 Have students work the following story problem using the map on this page. You are flying from Seattle to Chicago. About how many miles will you travel? (*1,850 miles*) If your plane

leaves Seattle at 7:30 P.M. and it takes 5 hours to get to Chicago, what time will it be when you arrive in Chicago? Remind students to consider the change in time zones before answering. (*7:30 P.M. + 5 hours = 12:30 A.M.; 12:30 A.M. + 2 hours for the time zone change = 2:30 A.M.*)

EXTENSION ACTIVITIES

◆ Have students make their own "Time Zone Calculator" using the blackline map of the United States on page T27. Instruct students to cut slits along the left- and right-hand sides of each clock-box at the top of the map. (*Students might prefer to cut out each box entirely*) Then have them cut a strip of paper ½ inch wide and about 30 inches long. Have them weave the strip through each box. Have them label the strip by writing 8:00, 9:00, 10:00, 11:00 in the boxes. (*Students should write one time in each box, starting in the box on the left and moving to the right.*) Have students slide the strip to the left so that 9:00 now shows in the Pacific Time Zone box. Have them write 12:00 in the Eastern Time Zone box. Have students continue to label additional times by sliding the strip to the left. Students can use this calculator to figure the time in all of the zones by sliding the strip to the right or to the left. You may wish to have students label the states on this map.

◆ Have students work in pairs to write story problems based on traveling in the United States between time zones. Then have students exchange story problems with other pairs of students and work the problems.

◆ Provide students with copies of the blackline map of North America on page T28. Have students find time zone maps of North America. Then have students label the countries and draw, color, and label the time zones in North America.

◆ Have students do research in encyclopedias to find out about daylight-saving time. Have the write a paragraph describing what it is and why was put into effect. Then have students find out if their state uses daylight-saving time.

◆ Have students make maps of the time zones Alaska and Hawaii. Compare these time zones with those in the continental United States.

AT HOME ACTIVITY

◆ Have students work with a family member to track the travels of their favorite sports team. Have them compute the time difference between the places where they play their out-of-town games and their hometown or city. They might make a table of their findings. Have them discuss how the time changes might affect the way the team plays.

OBJECTIVES

Students will

◆ use graph attack skills to read bar graphs, circle graphs, line graphs, and tables
◆ draw conclusions after reading bar graphs, circle graphs, line graphs, and tables

MATERIALS NEEDED

large circle cut into the same number of pieces as the number of students in the class
budget figures from the school board of your school district

VOCABULARY

bar graph   line graph
circle graph   table

INTRODUCING THE SKILL

◆ Have students conduct a poll on interests of class members, such as sports, TV shows, pets, books, etc. Tabulate the information and discuss with students the most appropriate way to present it. (*Students' answers may include the following: bar graph, line graph, circle graph, table.*)
◆ Have students bring to class examples of bar graphs, circle graphs, line graphs, and tables from newspapers and magazines. Discuss the information shown on each. Display the graphs on a bulletin board.

TEACHING NOTES

Page 84 Point out to students that the graph shows temperatures in increments of 10 degrees. Students need to estimate the temperatures between the increments. Have students practice estimating temperatures on the graph.
Page 85 Help students realize that bar graphs are drawings used to compare statistical information at a glance.
Page 86 Help students understand that a circle graph shows how a whole amount is divided into parts. Divide and cut a large circle into the same number of pieces as the number of students in the class. Give each student a piece. Ask students to color their piece of the circle according to which subject is their favorite: math—red, spelling—green, science—blue, social studies—purple, and reading—yellow. Collect the colored pieces and arrange the circle to show how the favorite subjects compare. Then help students figure what percent of the class chose each subject. Explain that in order to find the percentage, they need to divide the whole amount into each part. For example, if there are 28 students in the class and 7 chose reading as their favorite subject, then they would

divide 28 into 7 ($7 \div 28 = .25$ or 25%). Ask questions about the completed graph.
Page 87 Discuss with students that information can be presented in many different ways. Have them compare the precipitation map on page 42 with the graphs on pages 85 and 89. Have students compare the temperature map on page 43 with the graphs on pages 84 and 88.

EXTENSION ACTIVITIES

◆ Have students keep track of test scores in math, spelling, or another subject. Have them make bar graphs or line graphs to show their grades.
◆ Many newspapers publish daily weather maps and tables of high and low temperatures for the state and for the United States. Have students use this information to make bar graphs. Or have them track the information over a period of time and make line graphs.
◆ Have students use an encyclopedia, almanac, the annual *Statistical Abstract of the United States*, or other sources to find population data or other data for their state. Ask them to use the information to make a bar graph, circle graph, line graph, or table.
◆ Obtain budget figures from the school board of your school district. Have students make a circle graph showing how the school board spends the school district's money. Remind students that in order to find percentages, they must divide the whole amount into each category of spending. For example, if the whole amount of money spent is $350,000 and the amount of money spent on building maintenance is $115,000, then they would divide $350,000 into $115,000 ($115,000 \div \$350,000 = .328$ or about 33%).
◆ Obtain athletic schedules for local baseball games, soccer games, football games, or swim meets. Have students work in small groups to write questions about the schedules. Have the groups exchange questions and schedules and answer each other's questions.
◆ Have students make road mileage tables showing distances between places in their state, similar to the road mileage table on page 91. Students should use road atlases of their state to figure the distances.

AT HOME ACTIVITY

◆ Have students work with a family member to make a line graph comparing the costs of two expenses their family uses during a twelve-month period of time. They might graph the costs of natural gas, coal, oil, propane, electricity, water, phone, garbage, or other expenses. Have students and family members discuss their findings.

Letter to Families

Date _____

Dear Family:

Throughout the school year, your child will be learning about and practicing geography skills by using *Maps•Globes•Graphs, Level E*. In the twelve chapters, your child will learn to identify the North and South Poles, the Equator, the Prime Meridian, and the hemispheres on a map and globe. Your child will also work with map keys, directions, scale and distance, and latitude and longitude to interpret various kinds of maps. Some of these include route maps, relief and elevation maps, climate maps, and other maps. Your child also will study climate zones and time zones and will learn to understand and create various kinds of graphs and tables.

You can help your child reinforce what we study by asking him or her to talk to you about what we are doing. You might ask your child to explain to you some of the pictures and maps in the book.

You can help your child by engaging in the following activity at home to support and reinforce our study of these skills.

At least once each week watch an evening news program together and select one or two places around the world that are mentioned. Discuss with your child the climate at these places. Talk about how people dress to protect themselves in those climates. Ask your child to find examples in magazines and catalogs that show clothing that might be worn in those regions. Another time have your child find these places on a map and research the average rainfall and temperatures. Help your child make a chart or table showing this information for various places gathered over several weeks.

Thank you for your interest and support.

Sincerely,

_____

Carta a las Familias

Fecha _____

Estimada familia:

A lo largo de este año escolar, su hijo o hija aprenderá y practicará destrezas de geografía usando *Maps•Globes•Graphs*, *Level E.* En los doce capítulos, su hijo o hija aprenderá a identificar los polos Norte y Sur, el Ecuador, el Primer Meridiano y los hemisferios en un mapa y en el globo terráqueo. Su hijo o hija también trabajará con claves de mapas, direcciones, escala y distancia y latitud y longitud para interpretar diferentes tipos de mapas. Algunos de éstos incluyen mapas de rutas, mapas de relieve y elevación, mapas de clima y otros mapas. Su hijo o hija también estudiará las zonas climáticas y el huso horario y llegará a comprender y crear varios tipos de gráficas y tablas.

Usted puede ayudar a reforzar lo estudiado pidiendo a su hijo o hija que la cuente lo que hacemos en la escuela y que le explique algunos de los dibujos y mapas en el libro.

Usted puede ayudar a su hijo o hija en casa con la siguiente actividad:

Por lo menos una vez a la semana, vean juntos las noticias y elijan uno o dos lugares del mundo de los mencionados en el programa. Converse con su hijo o hija sobre el clima en esos lugares. Hablen de cómo la gente en esos lugares se viste para protegerse del clima. Pida a su hijo o hija que encuentre ejemplos en revistas y catálogos que muestren ropa que se puede usar en esas regiones. En otra oportunidad, pida a su hijo o hija que localice los lugares en el mapa e investigue la temperatura y lluvia promedio en cada uno. Ayude a su hijo o hija a mostrar en una gráfica o tabla la información que junte de distintos lugares a lo largo de varias semanas.

Gracias por su interés y apoyo.

Sinceramente,

_____

Name _____

MAP ATTACK!

✔ <u>Read the title.</u>

1. What is the title? _____

2. What is one thing you might learn from this map?

_____

✔ <u>Read the map key.</u>

3. Draw two symbols from the map in the boxes. Write their names on the lines below.

☐ _____ ☐ _____

✔ <u>Read the compass rose.</u>

4. Name something on the map in each direction.

North _____ South _____

East _____ West _____

✔ <u>Read the map scale.</u>

5. Use the map scale to measure the distance between two places on the map.

The distance from _____ to _____ is _____ miles.

✔ <u>Read the grid.</u>

6. How many squares are in each row? _____

7. How many squares are in each column? _____

8. Name one thing in A-1. _____

✔ <u>Draw a conclusion.</u>

9. Name one thing you learned from this map. _____

_____

Name _____

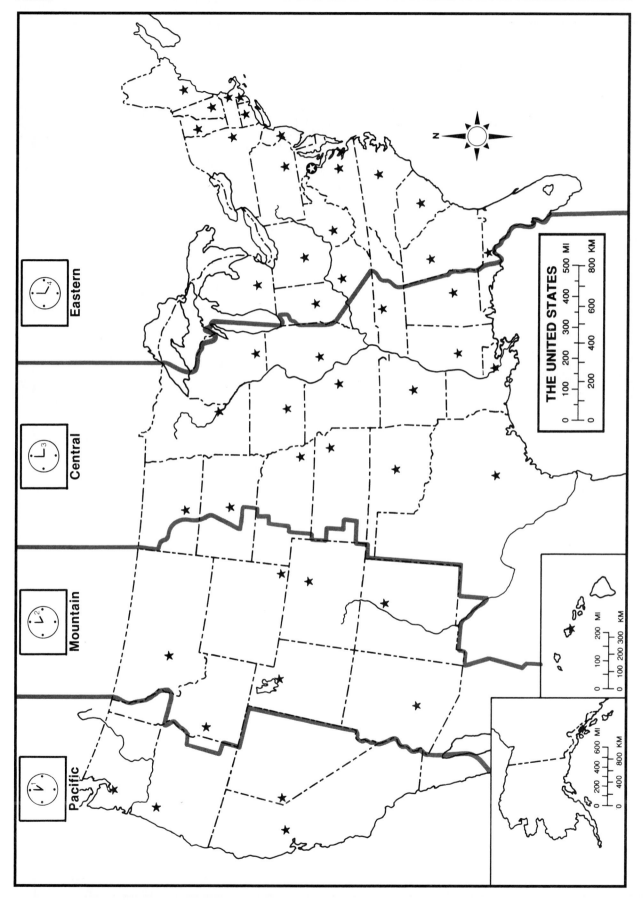

Eastern

Central

Mountain

Pacific

THE UNITED STATES

500 MI
400
300
200
100
0

800 KM
600
400
200
0

200 MI
100
0

200 KM
100
0

300

600 MI
400
200
0

800 KM
400
0

Name _____

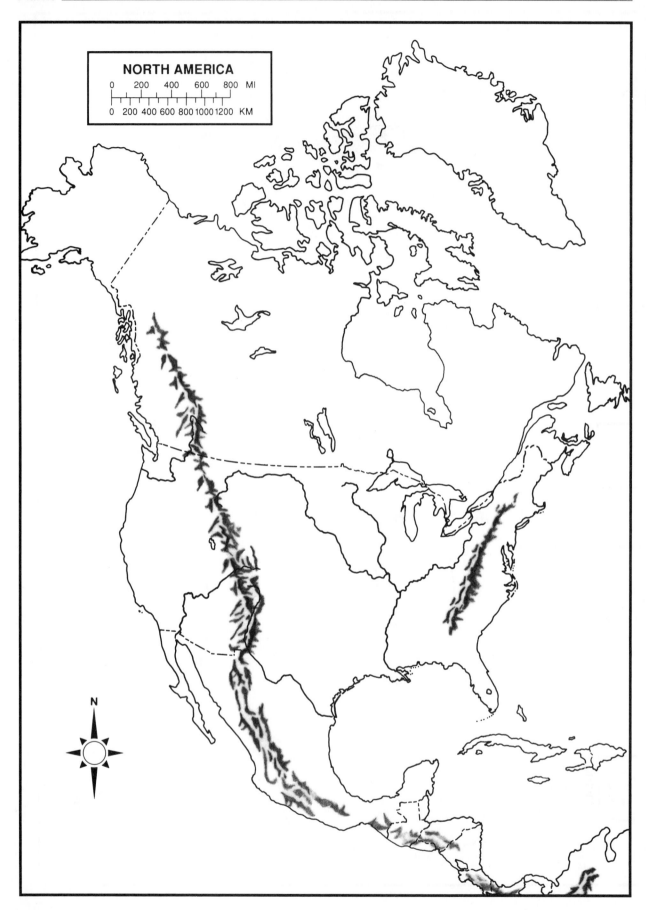

NORTH AMERICA

```
0    200   400   600   800  MI
0  200 400 600 800 1000 1200  KM
```

N

Name _____

SOUTH AMERICA

0   200   400   600 MI

0   200 400 600 800 KM

N

Name _____

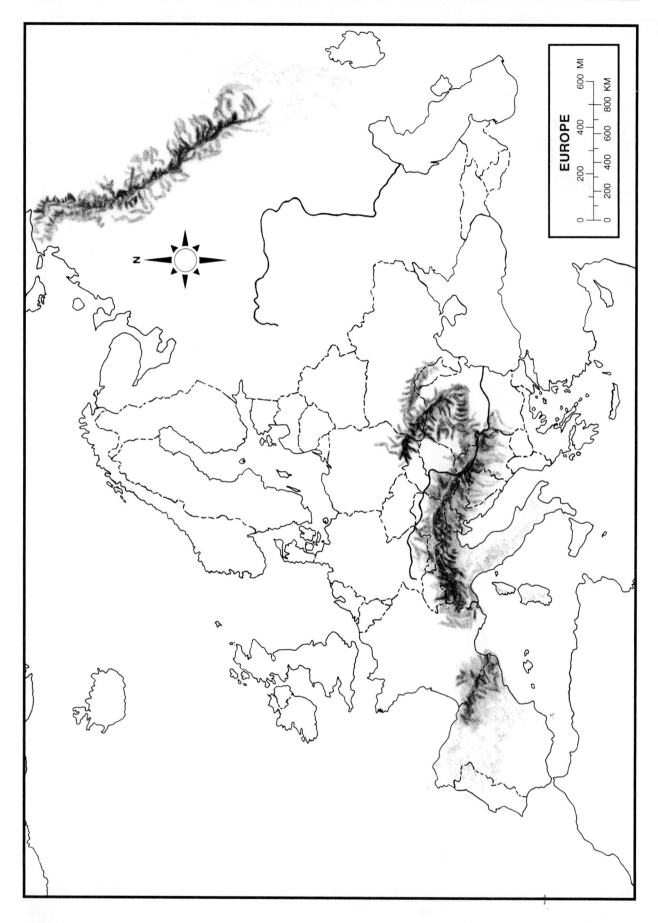

Name _____

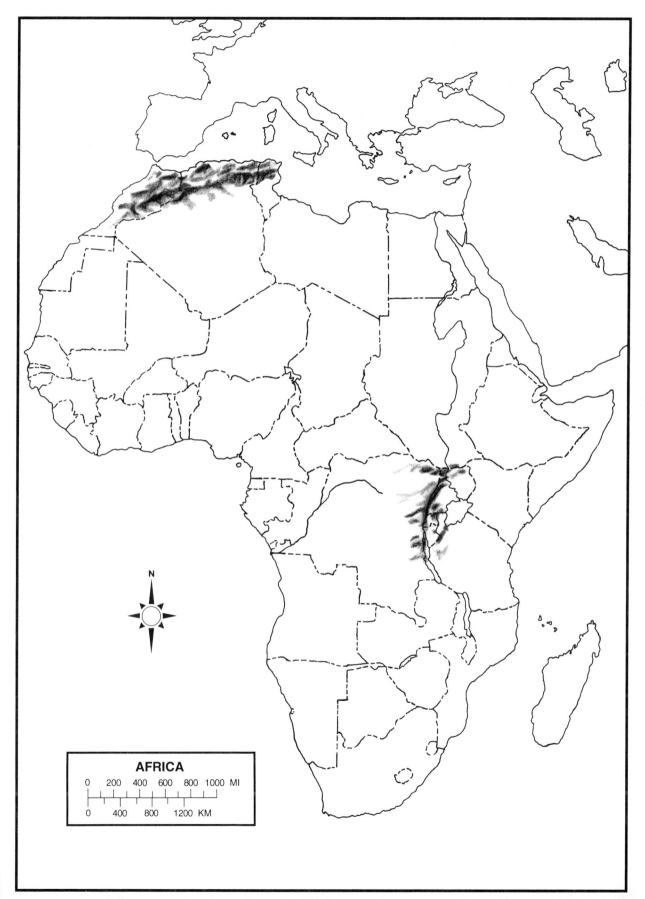

AFRICA

0   200   400   600   800 1000 MI

0   400   800   1200 KM

Name _____

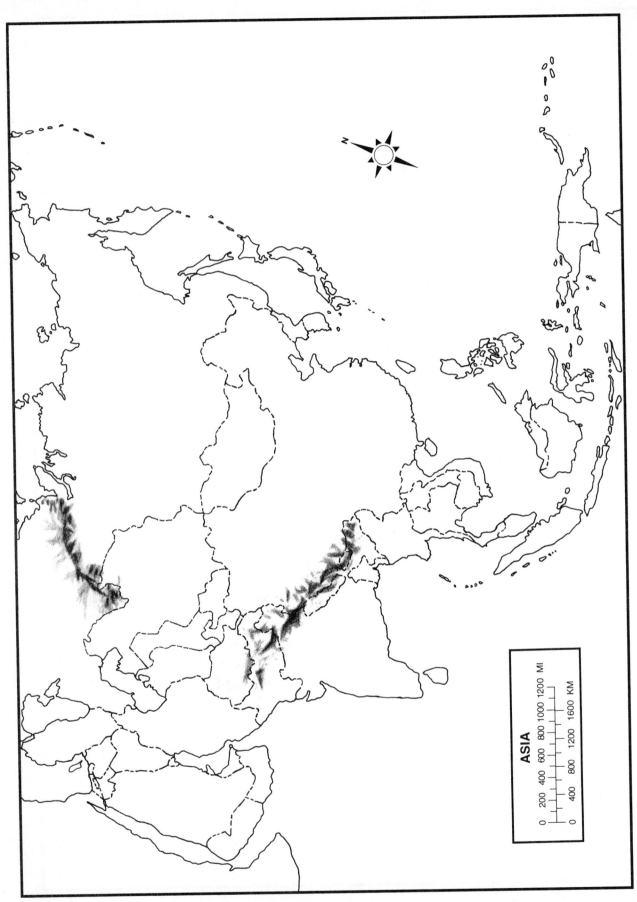

ASIA

1200 MI
1000
800
600
400
200
0

1600 KM
1200
800
400
0

Maps•Globes•Graphs Level E

Name _____

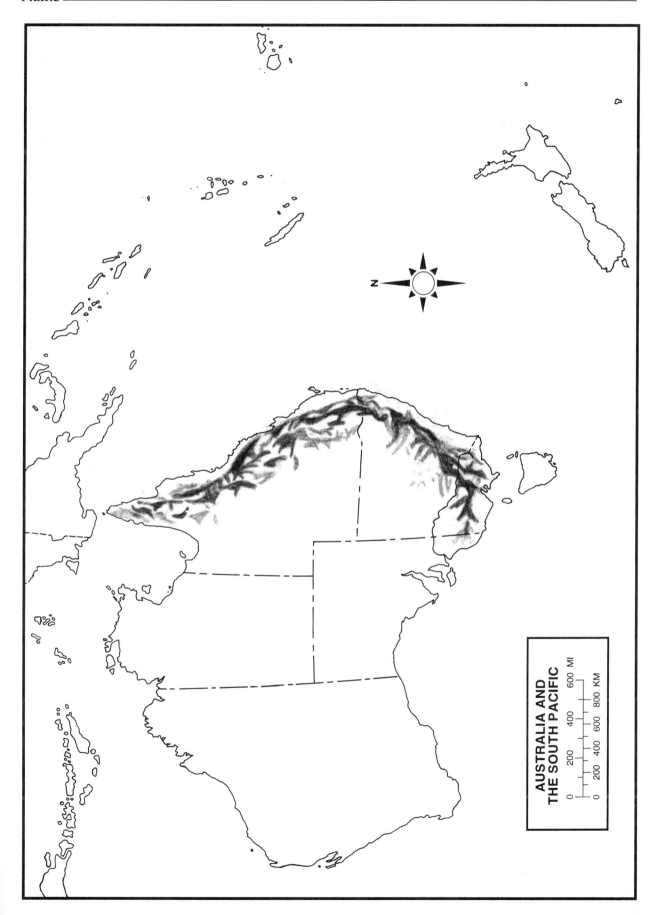

AUSTRALIA AND
THE SOUTH PACIFIC

600 MI
400
200
0

800 KM
600
400
200
0

Name _____

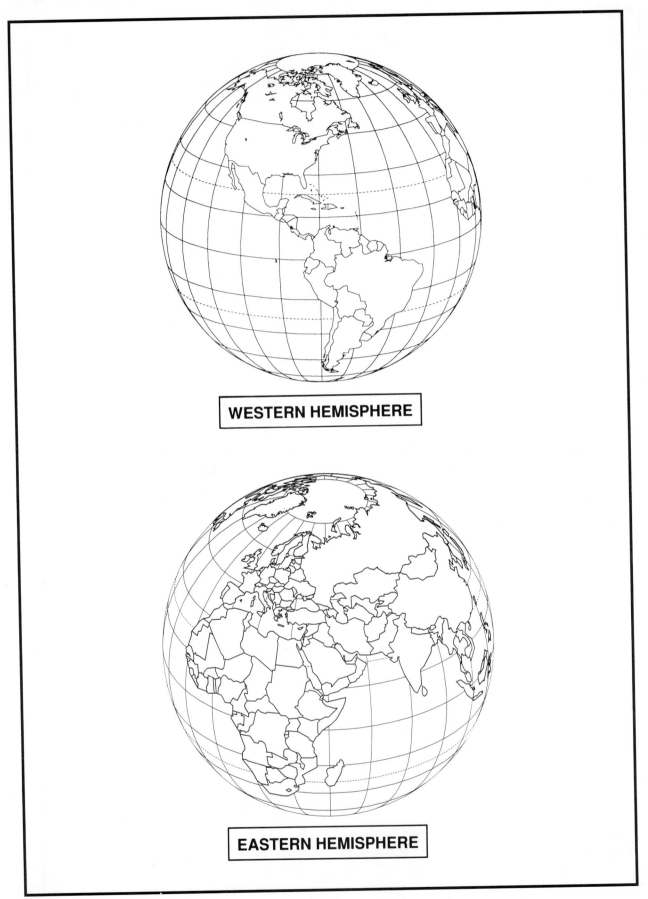

WESTERN HEMISPHERE

EASTERN HEMISPHERE

Name _____

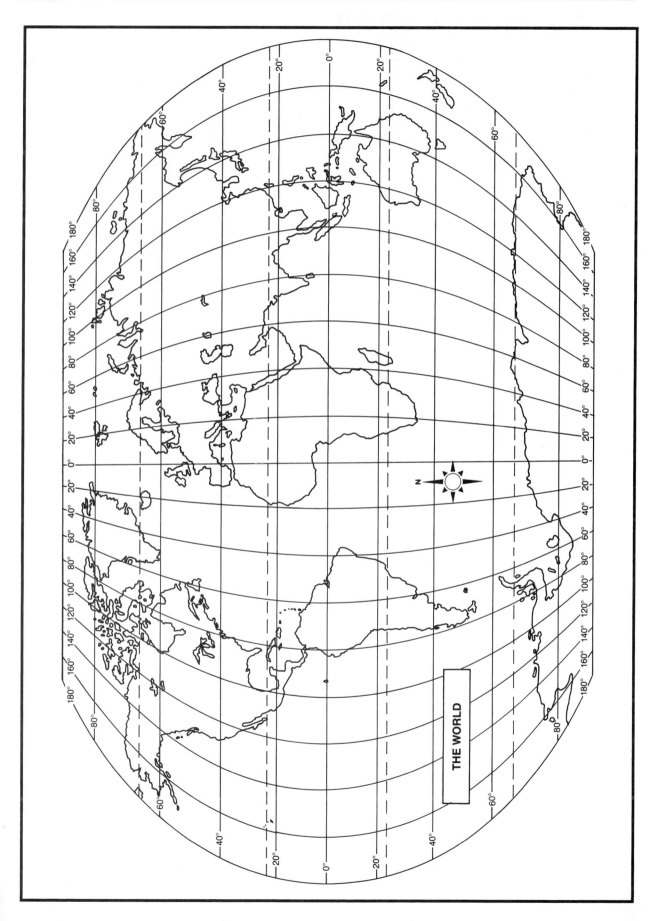

THE WORLD

Name _____

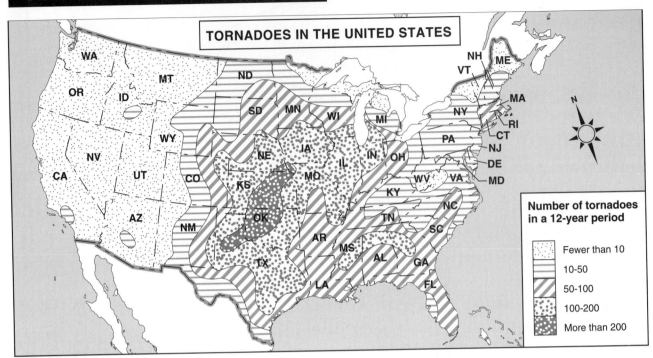

TORNADOES IN THE UNITED STATES

Number of tornadoes in a 12-year period

- Fewer than 10
- 10-50
- 50-100
- 100-200
- More than 200

1. **What is the special purpose of this map?**
   - (A) To show when tornadoes occur
   - (B) To show the strength of tornadoes
   - (C) To show how often tornadoes occur
   - (D) To show the damage caused by tornadoes

2. **Why do you think Iowa, Nebraska, Kansas, Oklahoma, and Texas are called "Tornado Alley"?**
   - (A) Tornadoes move in a straight line through this area.
   - (B) This area has more tornadoes than any other part of the United States.
   - (C) Tornadoes move through this area and die out when they hit the Rocky Mountains.
   - (D) Only a very narrow area is likely to have tornadoes.

3. **How many tornadoes generally occur in the northeast each year?**
   - (A) Fewer than 10
   - (B) 10-50
   - (C) 50-100
   - (D) More than 100

4. **Which of these states probably has the most tornadoes each year?**
   - (A) Kansas
   - (B) Missouri
   - (C) Nebraska
   - (D) Texas

5. **How many tornadoes generally occur along the gulf coast?**
   - (A) 10–50
   - (B) 50–100
   - (C) 100–200
   - (D) More than 200

6. **What overall conclusion can you draw from the map about tornado activity in the United States?**
   - (A) Only a few tornadoes occur in the Midwest.
   - (B) States located along a coast experience the most tornadoes.
   - (C) Tornadoes are most frequent in the southeast.
   - (D) The central part of the United States experiences the most tornadoes.

Maps•Globes•Graphs   Level E

Name _____

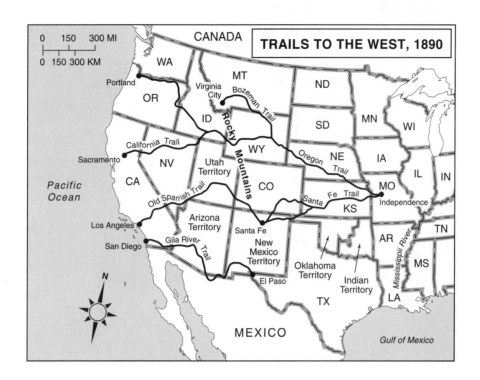

TRAILS TO THE WEST, 1890

7. **Which trail led to the northern Pacific Coast?**
   A Bozeman Trail
   B Gila River Trail
   C Old Spanish Trail
   D Oregon Trail

8. **Which trail crossed the border into Mexico?**
   A Bozeman Trail
   B Gila River Trail
   C Old Spanish Trail
   D Oregon Trail

9. **Which two trails would be used by pioneers who traveled from Independence, Missouri, to Los Angeles, California?**
   A Oregon Trail and Bozeman Trail
   B Oregon Trail and California Trail
   C Santa Fe Trail and Old Spanish Trail
   D Santa Fe Trail and Gila River Trail

10. **About how many miles long was a trip from Independence, Missouri, to Virginia City, Montana?**
    A 500
    B 800
    C 1,200
    D 2,000

11. **Which trail crosses only two states?**
    A Bozeman Trail
    B California Trail
    C Oregon Trail
    D Santa Fe Trail

12. **Which of the following best characterizes the Oregon Trail?**
    A It was the only trail that led to a state other than California.
    B It was the only trail that led to the state of Washington.
    C It was the easiest journey because it was the shortest and flattest route.
    D It was the hardest journey because it was the longest and most northern route.

Name _____

Use the city map below to answer the questions.

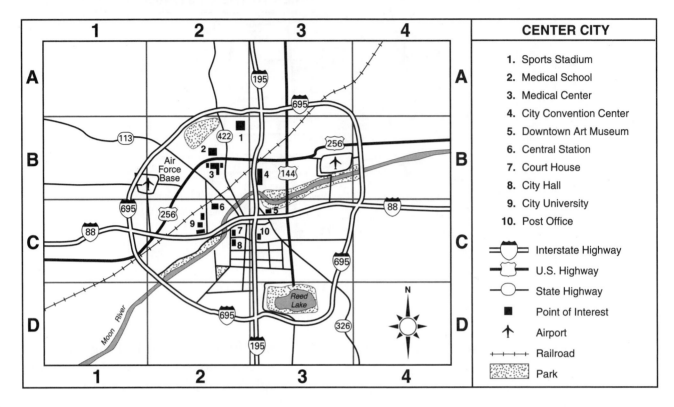

1. **In what grid square is the airport located?**
   - (A) A-3
   - (B) B-2
   - (C) B-3
   - (D) D-3

2. **Which two highways meet in the center of the city?**
   - (A) 256 and 88
   - (B) 422 and 113
   - (C) 195 and 88
   - (D) 195 and 695

3. **Which human feature is located in C-2?**
   - (A) 195
   - (B) The park along the river
   - (C) The air force base
   - (D) The river

4. **Which highway forms a loop around the city?**
   - (A) 326
   - (B) 422
   - (C) 88
   - (D) 695

5. **Which two buildings are located in grid square C-2?**
   - (A) Court House and City Hall
   - (B) Court House and Post Office
   - (C) City Convention Center and Central Station
   - (D) Downtown Art Museum and Central Station

6. **Which is the most direct route from downtown to the airport?**
   - (A) 256 to 88
   - (B) 195 to 256
   - (C) 88 to 695
   - (D) 88 to 144

Name _____

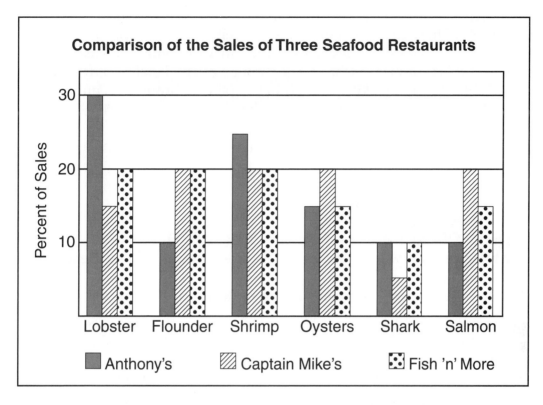

Comparison of the Sales of Three Seafood Restaurants

Percent of Sales

30

20

10

Lobster   Flounder   Shrimp   Oysters   Shark   Salmon

■ Anthony's   ▨ Captain Mike's   ⠿ Fish 'n' More

7. Sales of oysters make up about what percent of Anthony's sales?
- (A) 5%
- (B) 10%
- (C) 15%
- (D) 20%

8. What seafood item sells the most at Anthony's?
- (A) Shark
- (B) Lobster
- (C) Shrimp
- (D) Flounder

9. How do the sales of salmon compare between Anthony's and Captain Mike's?
- (A) Sales at both restaurants are about the same.
- (B) Anthony's sells about half as much salmon as Captain Mike's.
- (C) Anthony's sells twice as much salmon as Captain Mike's.
- (D) There is not enough information to compare.

10. What item sells the least at all the restaurants?
- (A) Lobster
- (B) Shrimp
- (C) Shark
- (D) Salmon

11. For which three types of seafood are sales at Fish 'n' More about the same?
- (A) Lobster, flounder, and shrimp
- (B) Lobster, flounder, and oysters
- (C) Oysters, shark, and salmon
- (D) Shrimp, oysters, and salmon

12. Which of the restaurants has the biggest difference between the highest sales and the lowest sales?
- (A) Anthony's
- (B) Captain Mike's
- (C) Fish 'n' More
- (D) There is not enough information given.

Standardized Tests/Answer Key

Level E of *Maps•Globes•Graphs* includes sample standardized tests on maps, globes, and graphs. These tests will familiarize students with formats and directions for taking standardized tests. The Midterm Test, found on pages T36 and T37, reviews skills learned in Chapters 1 through 6. The Final Test, found on pages T38 and T39, focuses on skills learned in Chapters 7 through 11, but also encompasses skills learned and practiced in earlier chapters.

When you administer the tests, pass along the following tips to students.

1. Read the directions for each page carefully.
2. Remember your **Map Attack!** skills.
3. Read each question carefully.
4. Decide which of the four answers is correct—A, B, C, or D.
5. Carefully fill in each answer circle completely. Press firmly with the pencil to make a dark mark.
6. If you finish the test before the time is up, go back and check your answers.

ANSWERS

Midterm Test

Page 36	1. C	2. B	3. B	4. A	5. B	6. D
Page 37	7. D	8. B	9. C	10. C	11. A	12. D

Final Test

Page 38	1. C	2. C	3. B	4. D	5. A	6. B
Page 39	7. C	8. B	9. B	10. C	11. A	12. A

Maps
Globes
Graphs

Steck Vaughn

Level E

Writer
Henry Billings

Consultants

Marian Gregory
Teacher
San Luis Coastal Unified School District
San Luis Obispo, California

Gloria Sesso
Supervisor of Social Studies
Half Hollow Hills School District
Dix Hills, New York

Norman McRae, Ph.D.
Former Director of Fine Arts and Social
Studies
Detroit Public Schools
Detroit, Michigan

Edna Whitfield
Former Social Studies Supervisor
St. Louis Public Schools
St. Louis, Missouri

Marilyn Nebenzahl
Social Studies Consultant
San Francisco, California

Karen Wiggins
Director of Social Studies
Richardson Independent School District
Richardson, Texas

Check the Maps•Globes•Graphs Website to find more fun geography activities at home.

Go to www.HarcourtAchieve.com/mggwelcome.html

Harcourt Achieve
Rigby • Steck-Vaughn

www.HarcourtAchieve.com
1.800.531.5015

Acknowledgments

Cartography

Land Registration and Information Service
Amherst, Nova Scotia, Canada

Gary J. Robinson

MapQuest.com, Inc.

R.R. Donnelley and Sons Company

XNR Productions Inc., Madison, Wisconsin

Photography Credits

COVER (globe, clouds): ©PhotoDisc; p. 4 ©Superstock; pp. 5, 6, 7(b) ©PhotoDisc; p. 7(a) ©Zuckerman/ PhotoEdit

Illustration Credits

Dennis Harms pp. 8, 56, 64, 70, 71, 72, 75; Michael Krone pp. 22, 86, 87; T.K. Riddle pp. 88, 89; Rusty Kaim p. 4

ISBN 0-7398-9105-7

© 2004 Harcourt Achieve Inc.

Printed in the United States of America.   8 030 11 10 09

Contents

Geography Themes

In *Maps•Globes•Graphs* you will learn about some of the tools that scientists use to study **geography**. Geography is the study of Earth, its features, and the ways people live and work on Earth. There are five **themes**, or main topics, to help people organize ideas as they study geography.

The Five Themes of Geography
- **Location**
- **Place**
- **Human/Environment Interaction**
- **Movement**
- **Regions**

Location

Location describes where something is found. You can name a location by using its address. Another way you can tell the location of something is by describing what it is near or what is around it. Location helps us learn where a certain lake is found, or how far a person from Maine must travel to get to Idaho.

 Look at this photograph. How would you describe the location of this home?

This home is located by a lake near a hill and woods.

Place

Place describes the kinds of features that make a location different from any other on Earth. **Physical features** are part of the natural environment. Some physical features are bodies of water, landforms, climate, soil, and plants and animals. **Human features** are developed or made by people. These features can include airports, buildings, highways, businesses, parks, and playgrounds.

The city in this photograph is Minneapolis, Minnesota. As you study the picture, look for physical and human features of Minneapolis.

 Use the physical and human features you find in the photograph and describe Minneapolis, Minnesota.

Answers will vary. Students should mention physical features such as trees,

and a river running through the city. They should also mention human features

such as buildings, roads, bridges, parks, and so on.

Human/Environment Interaction

Human/Environment Interaction describes how people affect the environment and how the environment affects people. This theme also explains how people depend on the environment. For example, people depend on the land for good soil to grow crops.

Human/Environment Interaction demonstrates how people adapt to their environment. It explains how people make changes to live in their surroundings.

 How do the people in these photographs adapt to the change of seasons in their climate?

In cold weather people wear heavy, warm clothing to keep them warm. In

warm or hot weather, people wear lighter-weight clothing to keep them

cool.

Human/Environment Interaction also considers how people change the environment to meet their needs and wants. Sometimes people change the course of a river to uncover flooded land or to bring water where it is needed.

 Look at the photograph of the dam shown here. How do you think changing the flow of a river's water might affect the plants and animals in the area?

Answers will vary. Students might mention that plant and animal life could

be affected by stopping the flow of water in one area and by flooding the

land in another area.

Movement

Movement explains how people, goods, information, and ideas move from place to place. The movement of people from other countries to settle in the United States is one example of movement. Another example is trade. Goods move across the country or around the world through trade. The spread of information and ideas through the Internet is another kind of movement.

Name two ways that people, goods, information, and ideas move from place to place.

Answers will vary, but may include railways, highways, rivers, airplanes,

pipelines, ships, trucks, telephones, newspapers, magazines, radio, and

television.

Information/Ideas

People/Goods

Both photographs above show movement. On the line below each picture write **People/Goods** if the picture shows movement of people and goods. Write **Information/Ideas** if the picture shows movement of information and ideas.

Regions

   Regions name areas that share one or more features. Physical features, such as landforms, natural resources, or climate can describe regions. Appalachia is a region in the eastern part of the United States defined by its physical feature— the Appalachian Mountains. Human features, such as land use, politics, religion, or language can also describe regions. Regions can be large or small.

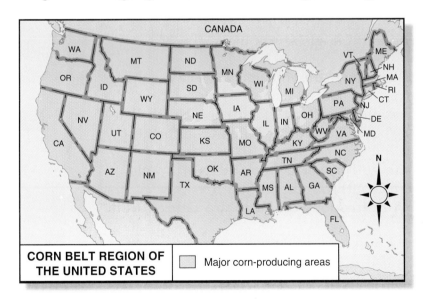

CORN BELT REGION OF THE UNITED STATES — Major corn-producing areas

Look at the map of the United States shown here. List the states that make up the Corn Belt. What makes the Corn Belt a region?

Corn Belt states: Iowa, Illinois, Nebraska, Minnesota, Indiana, Ohio, Wisconsin, Missouri, Michigan, South Dakota. Students should answer that The Corn Belt is a region defined by common land use—the growing of corn.

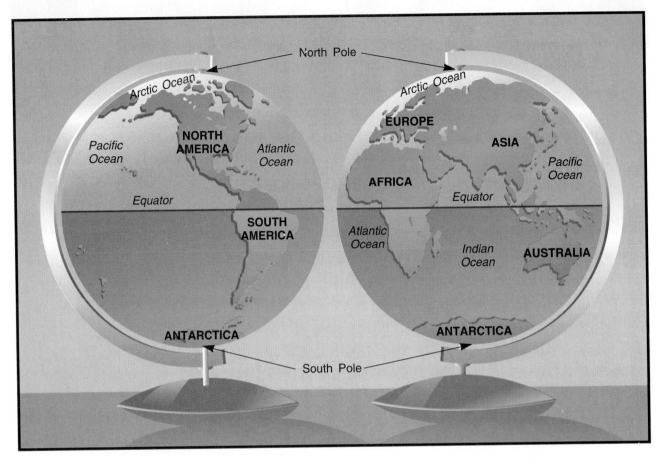

A globe is a model of Earth. Like Earth, a globe has the shape of a sphere, or ball.

The drawing above shows a globe. How can you find a place on the globe? One way is to know its direction. North America is located on the northern part of the globe. North is the direction toward the North Pole. Find the North Pole on the globe above. The **North Pole** is the farthest point north on Earth.

The South Pole is at the opposite end of Earth from the North Pole. The **South Pole** is the farthest point south on Earth. South is the direction toward the South Pole. All directions on Earth are figured from the North and South Poles.

Two other directions are east and west. North (N), south (S), east (E), and west (W) are called the **cardinal directions.** You know that once you are facing north, then east is always to your right. West is to your left. South is behind you. Knowing these directions will help you to find places. Practice using directions on the map above.

► South America is which direction from North America? south

► The Arctic Ocean is which direction from North America? north

► The Pacific Ocean is which direction from North and South America? west

► The Atlantic Ocean is which direction from North and South America? east

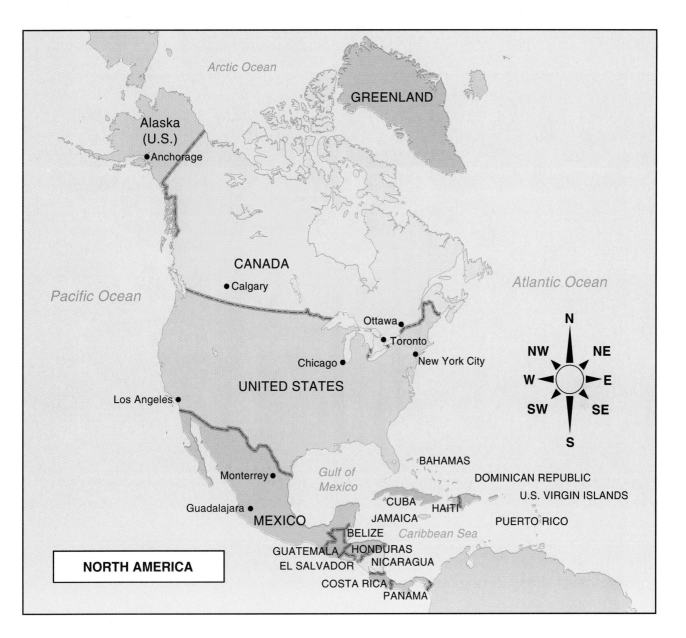

Maps have a special symbol to help you find directions. This symbol is called a **compass rose**. Look at the map above. Find the compass rose. North (N), south (S), east (E), and west (W) are all marked on the compass rose.

There are also other directions on the compass rose. These directions are in between the cardinal directions. They are called **intermediate directions**. The intermediate directions are northeast (NE), southeast (SE), northwest (NW), and southwest (SW). You need these to locate places that are between the cardinal directions

Find Chicago on the map. Find Toronto. What direction is Toronto from Chicago? It is between north and east, or northeast.

► Find Calgary on the map of North America above. In which direction would you travel from Calgary to reach Anchorage? NW

► From Monterrey, what direction is Guadalajara? SW

► From Los Angeles, what direction is Monterrey? SE

Using Directions on a Map

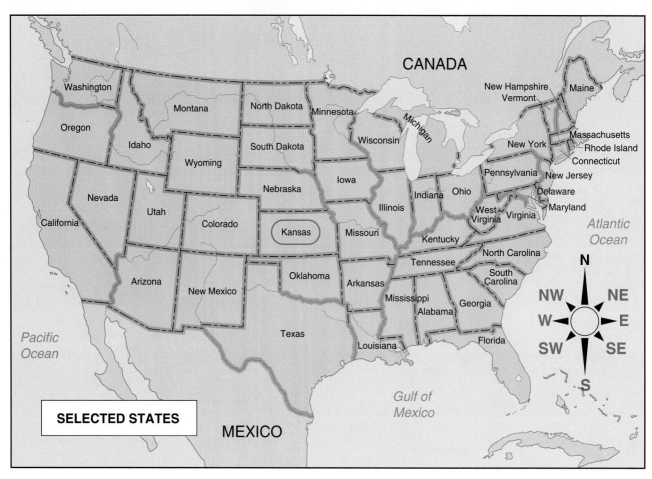

SELECTED STATES

1. Complete the compass rose on the map above. Add the missing cardinal directions. Then add the intermediate directions.

2. Find Kansas on the map. Circle the label.

   a. Which state is north of Kansas? _____ Nebraska _____

   b. Which state is south of Kansas? _____ Oklahoma _____

   c. Which state is east of Kansas? _____ Missouri _____

   d. Which state is west of Kansas? _____ Colorado _____

3. Which state is northeast of Utah? _____ Wyoming _____

4. Which state is southeast of Arkansas? _____ Mississippi _____

5. Which state is southwest of Illinois? _____ Missouri _____

6. Which state is northwest of Iowa? _____ South Dakota _____

7. What is west of California? _____ the Pacific Ocean _____

8. What is southeast of Texas? _____ the Gulf of Mexico _____

Using Directions on a Map

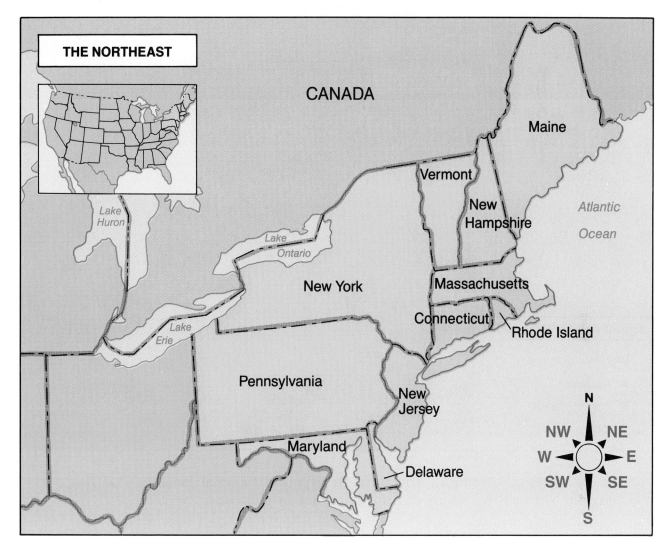

THE NORTHEAST

CANADA

Maine

Vermont

New Hampshire

Atlantic

Ocean

Lake Huron

Lake Ontario

New York

Massachusetts

Connecticut

Rhode Island

Lake Erie

Pennsylvania

New Jersey

Maryland

Delaware

N
NW   NE
W   E
SW   SE
S

1. Complete the compass rose. First add the cardinal directions. Then add the intermediate directions.

2. Write a direction to make each sentence true.

a. New Hampshire is _____ **north** _____ of Massachusetts.

b. Pennsylvania is _____ **south** _____ of New York.

c. New Jersey is _____ **southwest** _____ of Connecticut.

d. New Hampshire is _____ **north** _____ of Rhode Island.

e. Maine is _____ **east or northeast** _____ of New Hampshire.

3. Draw a conclusion. Find the small map of the United States above. It shows where the Northeast region of the United States is located. Why do you think this region is called the Northeast?

Answers will vary but may include the following:
The region is in the northeast corner of the United States.

Using Directions on a Map

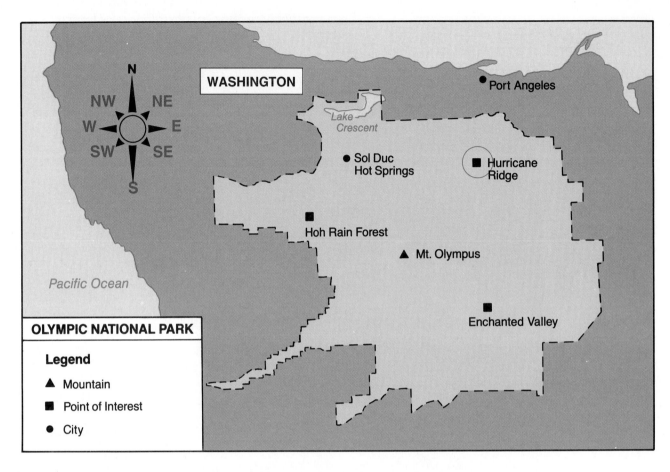

You are going on a camping trip through Olympic National Park in Washington. You will be hiking and do not want to get lost.

1. Complete the compass rose.
2. Your trip begins at Hurricane Ridge. It is in the northeast part of the park. Circle it on your map.

   What direction would you look to see Mt. Olympus? _____southwest_____
3. You will hike to Lake Crescent from Hurricane Ridge. What direction

   will you be walking? _____northwest_____
4. From Lake Crescent you will hike to Sol Duc Hot Springs. What

   direction will you be going? _____south_____
5. You want to camp in the Hoh Rain Forest. What direction do you hike

   from Sol Duc Hot Springs to the Hoh Rain Forest? _____southwest_____
6. What direction is the Pacific Ocean from the Hoh Rain Forest? ___west___
7. Your last stop will be at the Enchanted Valley. It is in the southeastern part of the park. What direction will you travel to get back to

   Hurricane Ridge from the Enchanted Valley? _____north_____

Skill Check

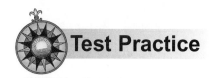 **Test Practice**

Vocabulary Check   compass rose   North Pole   intermediate directions
                        cardinal directions South Pole

Choose from the words above to make each sentence true.

1. North, south, east, and west are the _____cardinal directions_____ .

2. Directions on Earth are figured from the _____North Pole_____

   and the _____South Pole_____ .

3. Northwest and southeast are two of the _____intermediate directions_____ .

Map Check

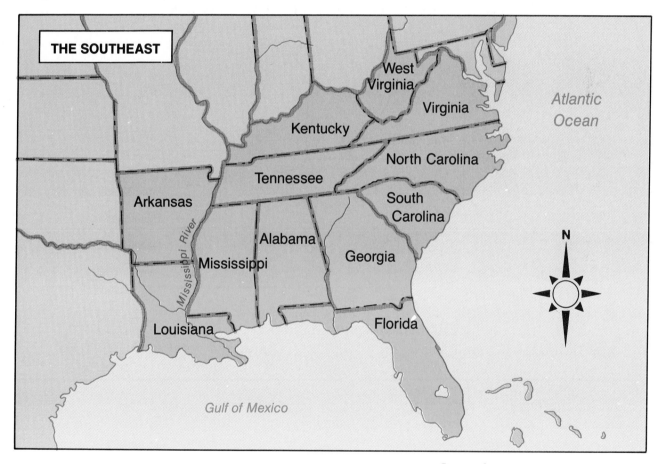

THE SOUTHEAST

West Virginia
Virginia
Kentucky
North Carolina
Tennessee
Arkansas
South Carolina
Alabama
Mississippi
Georgia
Louisiana
Florida
Mississippi River
Atlantic Ocean
Gulf of Mexico
N

1. What state is southwest of South Carolina? _____Georgia_____

2. What state is northeast of Kentucky? _____West Virginia_____

3. What direction is North Carolina from Tennessee? _____east_____

4. What two states are west of the Mississippi River? _____Arkansas_____

   and _____Louisiana_____

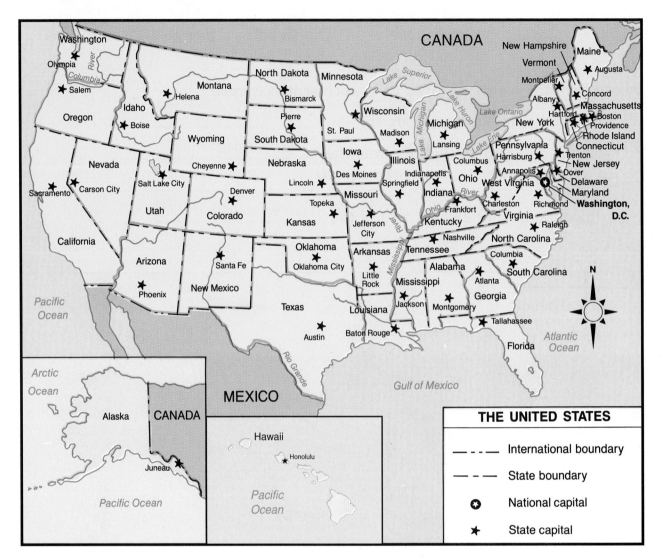

A **symbol** on a map represents something that is on Earth. Symbols can stand for cities, or mountains, or natural resources. To find the meaning of a symbol, read the legend. The **legend** explains what every symbol on the map means. We use the symbols and the legend to learn from the map.

Look at the legend above. Find the symbol for a state boundary. A **state boundary** shows where one state ends and another begins. Find a state boundary on the map.

Find the symbol for an international boundary in the legend. An **international boundary** shows where one country ends and another begins.

▶ Find your state on the map. What is the state capital? Answers will vary according to the
What states border your state? What are their capitals? state in which students live.

▶ Does your state have an international boundary? Answers will vary according
If so, what country shares a border with your state? to the state.

▶ What countries border the United States? Canada and Mexico

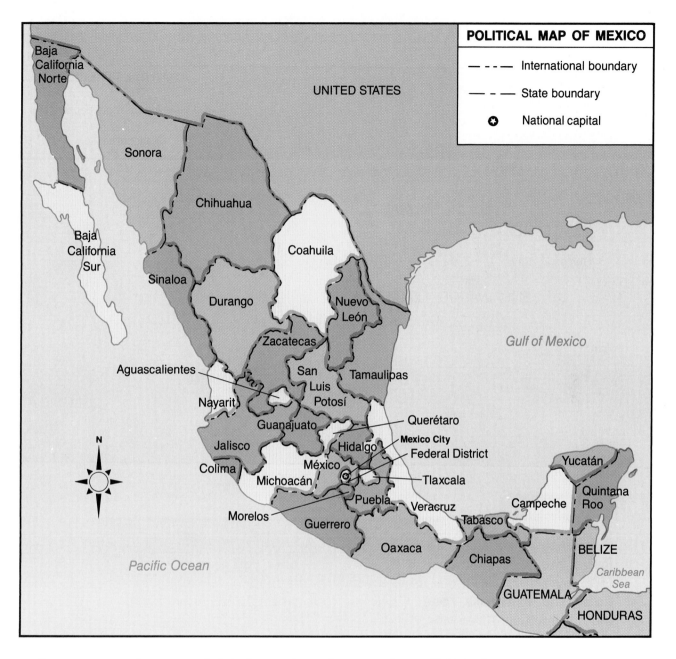

POLITICAL MAP OF MEXICO

— - -— International boundary

— - — State boundary

National capital

Some maps show special information about a place. Political maps show the boundaries separating states and countries. Other maps may show yearly rainfall or where people live. That is why the title is so important. The **title** tells you the purpose of the map.

Look at the title of the map above. It is a **political map** of Mexico. What can you expect to learn from this map? You can expect to find capital cities and state and international boundaries. The country of Mexico has 31 states. Like the United States, it has a national capital. Find the symbol for a national capital on this map and on the map on page 14.

► What city is the national capital of the United States? Washington, D.C.

► What city is the national capital of Mexico? Mexico City

► What country touches the northern international boundary of Mexico? United States

► Name two Mexican states along this boundary. Baja California Norte, Sonora, Chihuahua, Coahuila, Tamaulipas

Reading a Political Map

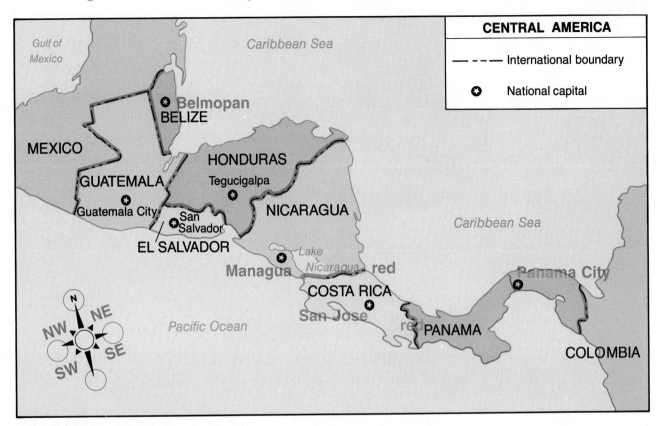

MAP ATTACK!

- **Read the title.** This map shows _____Central America_____.
- **Read the legend.** Check (✔) each symbol after you read its meaning. Check (✔) a matching symbol on the map.
- **Read the compass rose.** Circle the four cardinal directions. Label the intermediate directions.

1. Does this map show states or countries? _____countries_____

   How do you know? Answers will vary but may include the following: Boundaries are international. Each country has a national capital. Central America is a region made of countries.

2. Trace the borders of Costa Rica in red. What countries share a

   border with Costa Rica? _____Nicaragua, Panama_____

3. Write the capital city of each of these countries on the map where it belongs.

   | Panama City, Panama | San Jose, Costa Rica |
   | Managua, Nicaragua | Belmopan, Belize |

4. Draw a conclusion. What countries have coastlines on both the Caribbean Sea and the Pacific Ocean?

   Guatemala, Honduras, Nicaragua, Costa Rica, Panama

Reading a Political Map

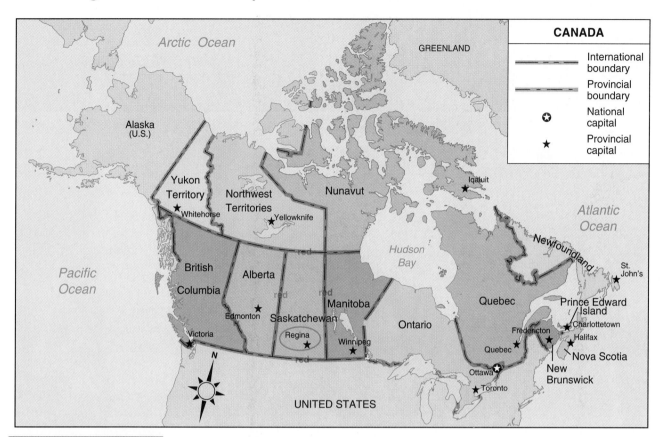

MAP ATTACK!

Follow the steps on page 16 to begin reading this map.

1. Canada is divided into ten provinces and three territories. The border lines look like state borders. Why is the border different between

   the Yukon Territory and Alaska? ___It is an international border.___

2. Circle the capital city of Saskatchewan. Write its name.

   _____Regina_____

3. Trace the borders of Saskatchewan in red.

   Which province is west of Saskatchewan? _____Alberta_____

   Which province is east of Saskatchewan? _____Manitoba_____

4. What is the national capital of Canada? _____Ottawa_____

5. Halifax is the capital of _____Nova Scotia_____.

6. Iqaluit is the capital of _____Nunavut_____

7. What is the capital of the Northwest Territories? _____Yellowknife_____

8. What is the capital of the Yukon Territory? _____Whitehorse_____

Reading a Political Map

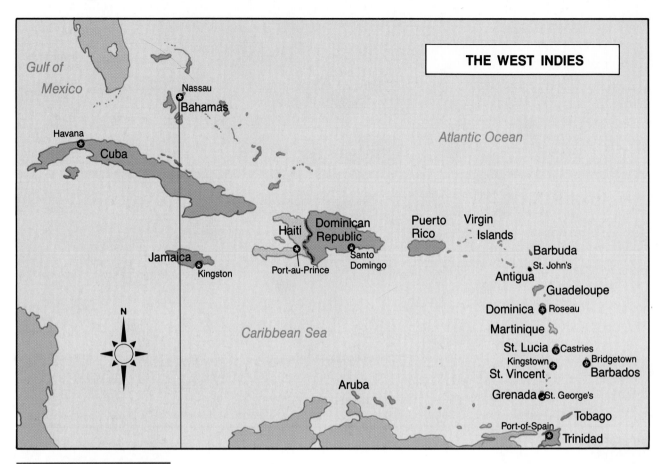

THE WEST INDIES

Gulf of Mexico

Nassau
Bahamas

Havana
Cuba

Atlantic Ocean

Jamaica
Kingston

Haiti
Port-au-Prince

Dominican Republic
Santo Domingo

Puerto Rico

Virgin Islands

Barbuda
St. John's
Antigua
Guadeloupe
Dominica ✪ Roseau
Martinique
St. Lucia ✪Castries
Kingstown ✪
St. Vincent
Bridgetown
Barbados
Grenada ✪St. George's

N

Caribbean Sea

Aruba

Tobago
Port-of-Spain
Trinidad

MAP ATTACK!

Follow the steps on page 16 to begin reading this map.

1. Find the island that is divided into two separate countries. Name each country and its capital.

   a. _____ **Haiti, Port-au-Prince** _____

   b. _____ **Dominican Republic, Santo Domingo** _____

2. Locate the Bahamas on the map above. Nassau is the capital city of the Bahamas. Draw a line south from Nassau to the bottom of the map.

   What countries do you cross? _____ **Cuba, Jamaica** _____

3. Write the intermediate direction that makes each sentence true.

   a. Martinique is _____ **northwest** _____ of Barbados.

   b. Trinidad and Tobago are _____ **southeast** _____ of Puerto Rico.

   c. Guadeloupe is _____ **northeast** _____ of Aruba.

4. Draw a conclusion. The West Indies form the northern and eastern boundary of what sea? _____ **Caribbean Sea** _____

Skill Check

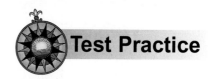

Vocabulary Check   symbol   legend   title

boundaries   political map

Use each word or phrase to finish a sentence.

1. A _____political map_____ shows the boundaries that separate different states or countries.

2. The map _____title_____ tells you what the map is about.

3. Lines that separate states or countries are _____boundaries_____.

4. The _____legend_____ tells you what the symbols on a map mean.

5. A _____symbol_____ on a map can stand for a city, a mountain, or a resource.

Map Check

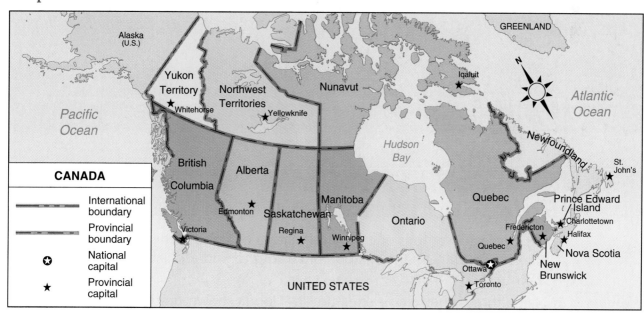

Match the capital with the province.

1. __B__ Toronto   A. Manitoba

2. __E__ Edmonton   B. Ontario

3. __A__ Winnipeg   C. Quebec

4. __C__ Quebec   D. Nova Scotia

5. __F__ Victoria   E. Alberta

6. __D__ Halifax   F. British Columbia

Geography Themes Up Close

Place is a location that has physical and human features that set it apart from other locations. Physical features can include bodies of water, landforms, climate, and plants and animals. Human features can include the kind of government, customs, art, buildings, and other things made by people. The map below shows Florida and some of its features.

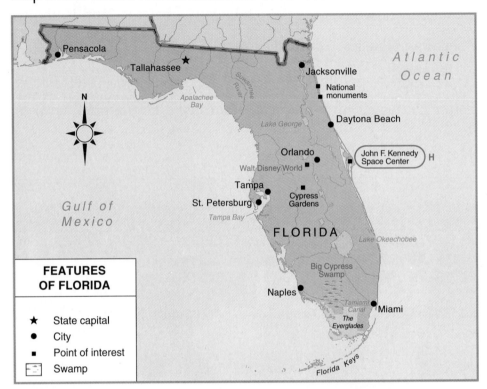

1. Big Cypress Swamp is one physical feature of Florida. This swamp is east of Naples, Florida. Use the symbol for swamp to find and label Big Cypress Swamp on the map.

2. Name three other physical features of Florida shown on the map.

   Any three physical features shown on the map besides Big Cypress

   Swamp. Examples: The Everglades, Suwannee River, lakes, bays,

   Florida Keys

3. The John F. Kennedy Space Center was set up in 1964 as a launch site for space missions. It is on the coast southeast of Daytona Beach. Circle this feature on the map. Then, mark **P** next to the circle if it is a physical feature. Mark **H** if it is a human feature.

4. Walt Disney World, near Orlando, is a human feature of Florida. Use the Point of Interest symbol in the legend to find Walt Disney World. Then, label it on the map.

FEATURES OF OTTAWA, ONTARIO

- –·–·– Province boundary
- —— City boundary
- 🍁 Trans-Canada highway
- ⑯ Provincial route
- ▪ Point of interest
- ← Airport
- ▨ Park

5. The Ottawa River forms the northwestern border of Ottawa. Label the Ottawa River. Then, mark **P** next to your label if it is a physical feature. Mark **H** if it is a human feature.

6. Name two physical features of Ottawa. Any two of the following:

   Rideau River, Rideau Falls, Dow's Lake

7. The Rockcliffe Airport is a human feature in the northeast corner of Ottawa. Use the airport symbol in the legend to find Rockcliff Airport. Then, label it on the map.

8. What are two other human features of Ottawa?

   Any two of the following: Supreme Court, Parliament Building, National Library, railroad station, Prime Minister's house, City Hall, University of Ottawa, Museum of Science and Technology, Ottawa International Airport, roads

9. Describe how the features of Ottawa differ from the town or city where you live.

   Answers will vary. Accept all reasonable answers.

3 Scale and Distance

A **map scale** compares distance on a map with distance in the real world. We use a map scale to find the distance between two places. A map scale shows distance in both **miles** (MI) and **kilometers** (KM). It looks like this:

```
0       220      440 MI
|--------|--------|
0       350      700 KM
```

▶ What do the letters MI and KM stand for? miles, kilometers

▶ Which distance is longer, 400 miles or 400 kilometers? 400 miles

Look at the map of the United States on page 23. Suppose you want to find the distance between Los Angeles and New York City. You will need a ruler, a pencil, and a piece of paper.

Here is how you use the map scale.

Step 1 Using your ruler, measure the distance between Los Angeles and New York City. On this map, Los Angeles and New York are 5½ inches apart.

Step 2 Look at the map scale in the lower right-hand corner. You can see that 1 inch equals 440 miles. Remember, there are 5½ inches between Los Angeles and New York City. Use multiplication to find the distance in miles or kilometers.

$$
\begin{array}{lr}
\text{number of miles per inch} & 4\,4\,0 \\
\times \text{ number of inches} & \times \quad 5.5 \\
\hline
= \text{distance in miles} & 2\,4\,2\,0
\end{array}
$$

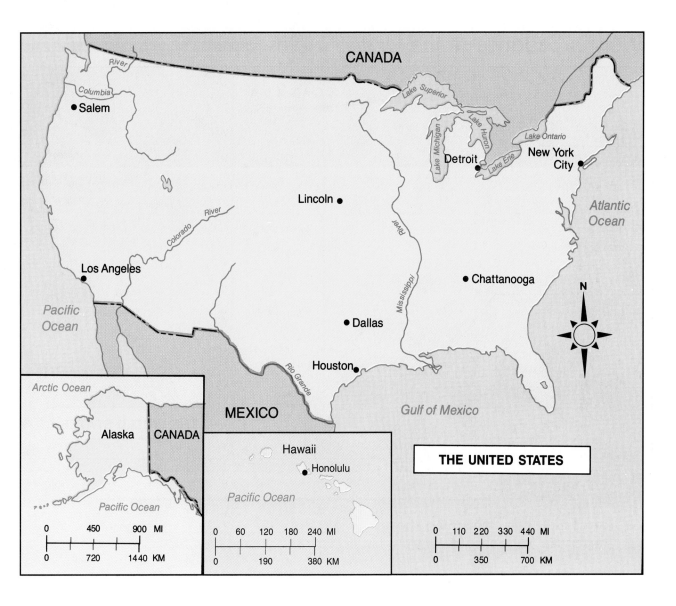

Look at the map of the United States above. Find the two smaller maps in the left-hand corner. One shows Alaska and the other shows Hawaii. Alaska and Hawaii are far from the other forty-eight states. This map isn't big enough to show where Alaska and Hawaii really are. So they are shown in inset maps.

An **inset map** is a small map within a larger map. An inset map may have its own scale. Map scales change depending on how much area is shown. Compare the map scales on the inset maps with the large map.

► One inch equals how many miles on the map of Hawaii? 240 miles

► One inch equals how many miles on the map of Alaska? 900 miles

► What can you tell about the sizes of Alaska and Hawaii? Alaska is larger than Hawaii.

► To figure the distance between Dallas and Houston, which map scale do you use? the United States map scale

► What is the distance between Dallas and Houston? about 220 miles

► Can you figure the distance between Honolulu and Los Angeles using these maps? Why or why not? No, because the space between Honolulu and Los Angeles is not shown on the maps.

Figuring Distance in the United States

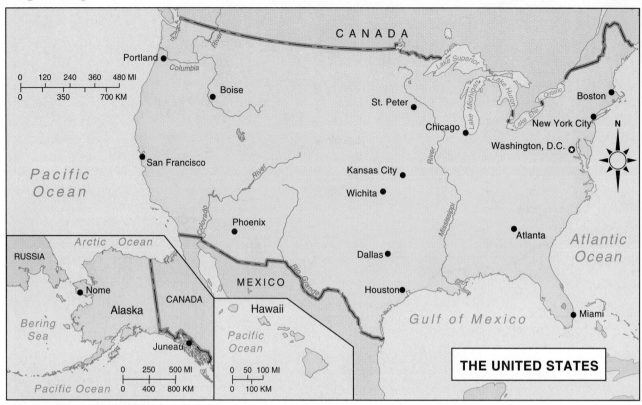

MAP ATTACK!

- **Read the title.** This map shows _____the United States_____.
- **Read the map scale.** On the large map, one inch stands for

_____480_____ miles.

Use your ruler to figure these distances.

1. What two states are shown in the inset maps above? _____Alaska_____

   and _____Hawaii_____   All answers here are approximate.

2. From Phoenix to Kansas City is about _____960_____ miles.

3. From New York City to Washington, D.C. is about _____240_____ miles.

4. From Kansas City to Boston is about _____1200_____ miles.

5. From Nome to Juneau is about _____1000_____ miles.

6. Is it farther from San Francisco to Houston or from Portland to Chicago?

   _____Portland to Chicago_____

Figuring Distance in the Great Lakes States

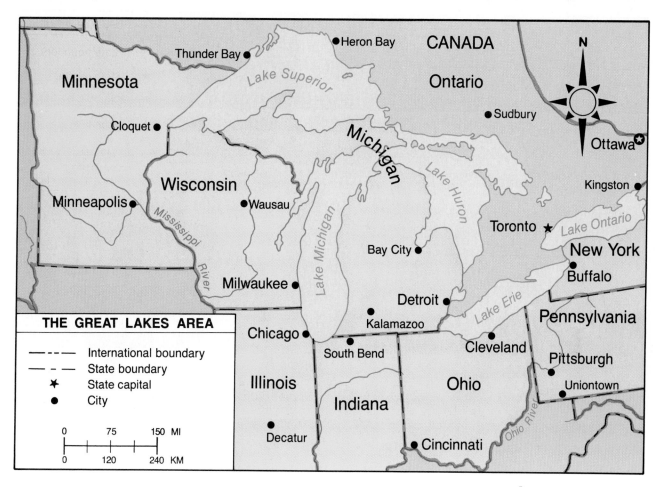

Use your ruler to figure these distances.

All answers here are approximate.

1. From Chicago to Decatur is about __150__ miles.

2. From Wausau to Milwaukee is about __150__ miles.

3. From Thunder Bay to Minneapolis is about __290__ miles.

4. From Toronto to Buffalo is about __75__ miles.

5. From Cleveland to Heron Bay is about __525__ miles.

6. From Milwaukee to Ottawa is about __600__ miles.

7. From Sudbury to Detroit is about __300__ miles.

8. From Ottawa to Cincinnati is about __600__ miles.

9. Is it farther from Chicago to Sudbury or from Heron Bay to Cleveland?

   Heron Bay to Cleveland

10. Is it farther from Ottawa to Kingston or from Milwaukee to Chicago?
    The distances are the same. (Depending on the points of measurement, one pair of cities may appear to be farther apart than the other.)

Figuring Distance on a State Map

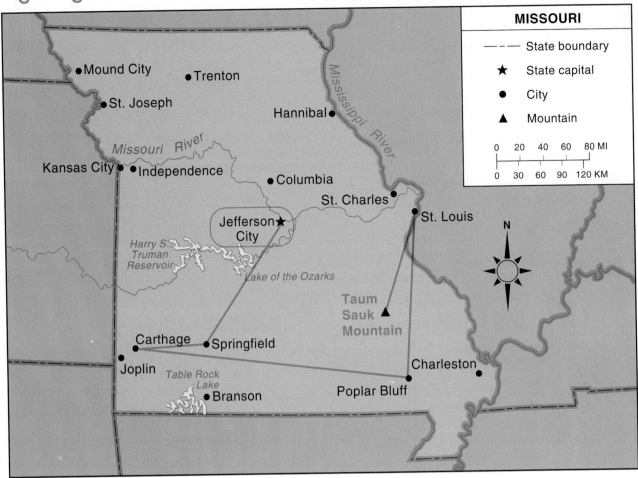

Imagine you are going on a tour of Missouri. Use a ruler to draw lines as you figure these distances and directions.

1. Find the state capital on the map. Circle it.

   a. What direction will you go from the state capital to Springfield? __SW__

   b. From the state capital to Springfield is about __120__ miles.

2. a. What direction will you go from Springfield to Carthage? __W__

   b. From Springfield to Carthage is about __60__ miles.

3. a. What direction will you go from Carthage to Poplar Bluff? __SE__

   b. From Carthage to Poplar Bluff is about __240__ miles.

4. a. What direction will you go from Poplar Bluff to St. Louis? __N__

   b. From Poplar Bluff to St. Louis is about __140__ miles.

5. There is a mountain about 80 miles southwest of St. Louis and about 60 miles northwest of Poplar Bluff. Find it on the map. Label it Taum Sauk Mountain. You have reached the highest point in Missouri!

Skill Check

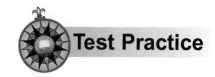

Vocabulary Check   map scale   miles   kilometers   inset map

Use each word or phrase to finish a sentence.

1. A map scale shows distance in _____ miles _____ and
   _____ kilometers _____ .

2. A small map within a larger map is called an _____ inset map _____ .

3. A _____ map scale _____ is used to compare distance on a map with
   distance on Earth.

Map Check

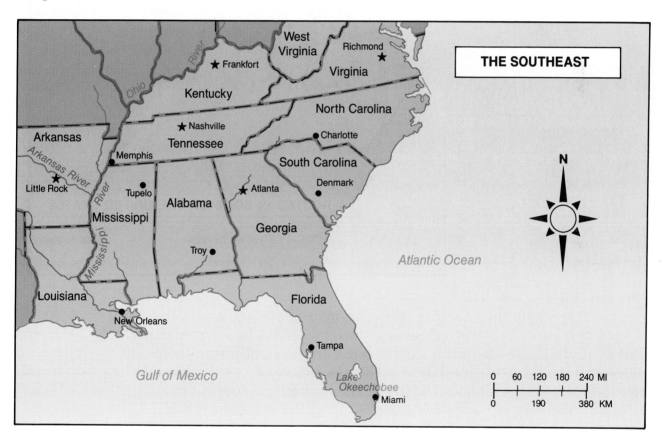

Use a ruler and the map scale to figure these distances.   **All answers here are approximate.**

1. From Atlanta to Richmond is about __480__ miles.

2. From Memphis to Frankfort is about __360__ miles.

3. From Nashville to Miami is about __840__ miles.

4. Is it farther from Nashville to New Orleans or from Nashville to

   Richmond? _____ Nashville to Richmond _____

4 🌐 Route Maps

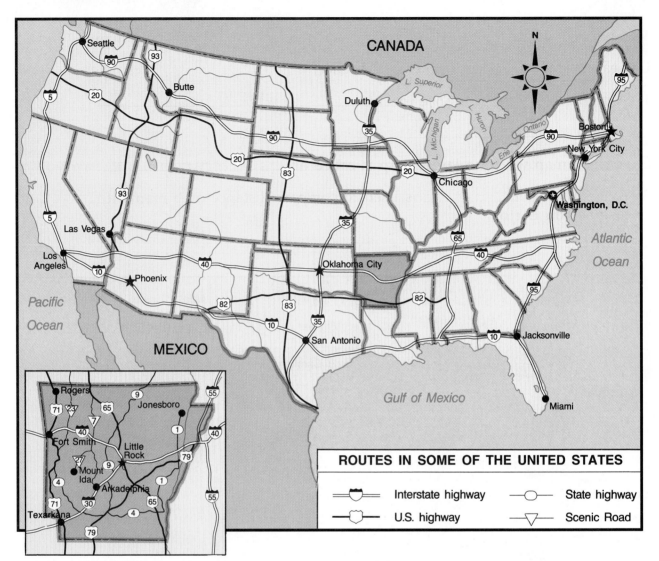

ROUTES IN SOME OF THE UNITED STATES

| ──🛡️── Interstate highway | ──○── State highway |
| ──🛡️── U.S. highway | ──▽── Scenic Road |

Some maps help us to plan a trip. The map above shows several kinds of routes. A **route** is a way of getting from one place to another. Each kind of route is shown in the legend. Find the symbol for an interstate highway in the legend. **Interstate highways** usually cross the country from one side to the other. Find an interstate highway on the map.

A **U.S. highway** crosses several states. Find the symbol for a U.S. highway in the legend. Then find a U.S. highway on the map.

State highways connect cities and towns within one state. **Scenic roads** cross areas that offer a beautiful view. Find the symbols for state highway and scenic road. Look at the inset map of Arkansas. What kinds of routes do you see? interstate highways, U.S. highways, state highways, scenic roads

▶ Interstate 35 connects what northern city with what southern city? Duluth, San Antonio

▶ U.S. 93 connects Las Vegas with the boundary of what country? Canada

▶ What state highway crosses southern Arkansas? Highway 4

▶ Where are the scenic roads in Arkansas? in the northwestern part of the state (7, 23, 27)

▶ What U.S. highway passes through Little Rock? U.S. 65

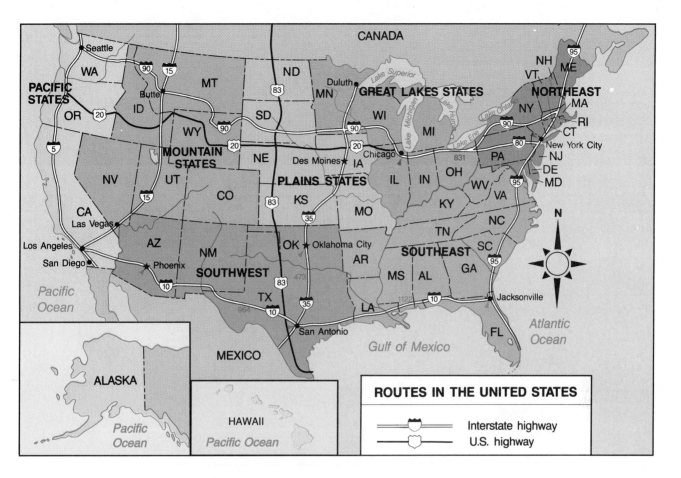

Look at the route map above. It shows interstate and U.S. highways crossing regions of the United States. A **region** is an area with many things in common. Find the Pacific States. Notice that all of the Pacific States touch the Pacific Ocean. What states are included in this region?

Three regions are named for intermediate directions. Find them. Name the states in the Southwest, the Southeast, and the Northeast.

Three regions are named for land or water forms. Find them. Name the states in the Mountain States, the Plains States, and the Great Lakes States.

Route maps often show the distance between cities. Find the small red triangle pointing to Chicago. That triangle is a **mileage marker**. The next mileage marker east of Chicago is in New York City. The distance from Chicago to New York City is 831 miles. Find the red number 831 near the route from Chicago to New York City.

► What lakes border the Great Lakes States? Lake Superior, Lake Michigan, Lake Huron, Lake Erie

► What regions does Interstate 10 cross? Pacific States, Southwest, Southeast

► What regions does U.S. 83 cross? Plains States, Southwest

► What interstate crosses the Mountain States from north to south? Interstate 15

► What U.S. highway crosses the Plains States from north to south? U.S. 83

► What highways would take you from Seattle to Las Vegas via (by way of) Butte? Interstates 90 and 15

► What is the distance from San Antonio to Jacksonville? 1122 miles

Reading a Route Map

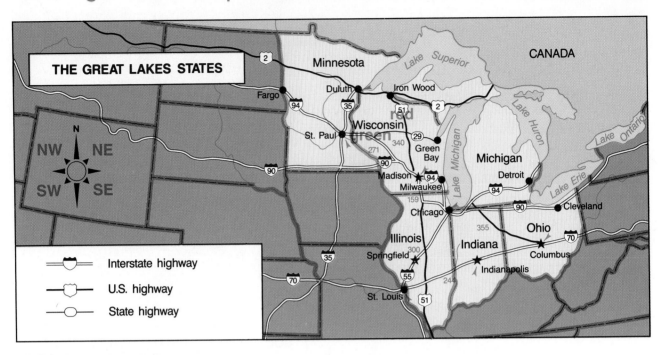

MAP ATTACK!

- **Read the title.** This map shows ____the Great Lakes States____ .

- **Read the legend.** The three types of highways shown are __U.S.__ ,
  ____state____ , and ____interstate____ .

- **Read the compass rose.** Label the intermediate directions.

1. What states are included in this region? ____Minnesota, Wisconsin,____
   ____Illinois, Indiana, Michigan, Ohio____

2. Which of the Great Lakes border this region?
   ____Lake Superior, Lake Michigan, Lake Huron, Lake Erie____

3. Trace the route from Green Bay to St. Paul. Use a green pencil or
   marker. What highways would you take? ____29, I-94____

4. Trace the route from Green Bay to Duluth via Iron Wood. Use a red
   pencil or marker. What highways would you take? ____29, 51, 2____

5. Is it farther from Chicago to St. Louis or from Chicago to Columbus?
   ____Chicago to Columbus____

6. Where would you see this sign?

Duluth	340
St. Paul	271
Chicago	159

   ____in Madison____

Reading a Route Map

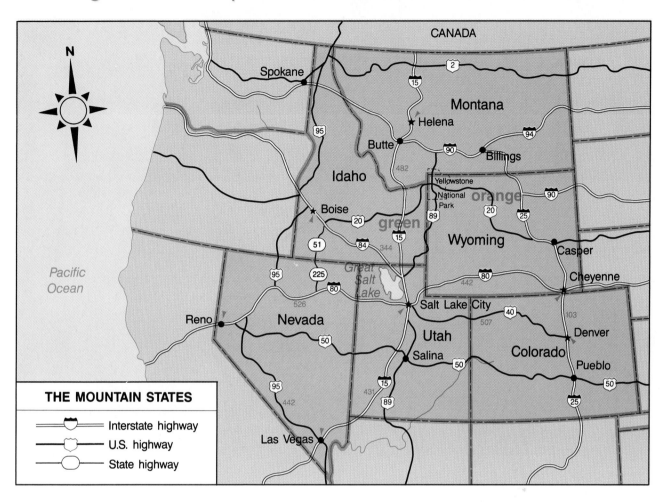

1. What region is shown here? _____the Mountain States_____

2. What states are in this region? _____Montana, Idaho, Wyoming,_____
   _____Nevada, Utah, Colorado_____

3. Trace the route from Helena to Salt Lake City in green.

   a. What highway takes you from Helena to Salt Lake City? _____I-15_____

   b. How many miles is it from Helena to Salt Lake City? _____482_____

   c. What states do you cross? _____Montana, Idaho, Utah_____

4. Trace the route from Helena to Cheyenne in orange. Be sure to go through Yellowstone National Park.

   What highways would you take? _____I-15, I-90, U.S. 89, U.S. 20, I-25_____

5. What U.S. highway connects Interstate 84 with Interstate 80? _____95_____

6. Where would you see this sign? | U.S. 95 ↑ / ← I-15 → | _____in Las Vegas_____
   (I stands for Interstate.)

Figuring Distance on a Route Map

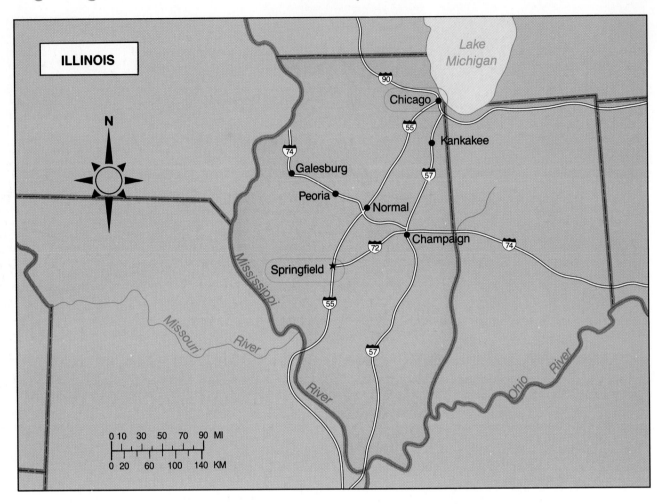

1. Circle the capital of Illinois on the map. Name it. _____Springfield_____
2. Chicago is the largest city in Illinois. Find it on the map and circle it.

   All answers here are approximate.

3. From Chicago to Springfield is about _____180_____ miles.
4. You want to find the shortest route from Chicago to Springfield. Would you drive Interstate 57 and Interstate 72 or Interstate 55 through

   Normal? _____Interstate 55 through Normal_____

   What direction would you be traveling? _____southwest_____

5. From Kankakee to Champaign is about _____90_____ miles.

   What direction is Champaign from Kankakee? _____southwest_____

6. From Springfield to Champaign is about _____80_____ miles.

   What direction is Champaign from Springfield? _____northeast_____

7. If you drove 40 miles an hour from Springfield to Champaign, how many

   hours would it take? _____about two hours_____

Skill Check

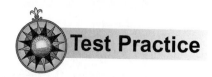

Test Practice

Vocabulary Check

route
state highway
mileage marker

interstate highway
scenic road

U.S. highway
region

1. An _____ interstate highway _____ crosses the entire country.

2. A _____ U.S. highway _____ crosses several states.

3. To figure distances on route maps, use the _____ mileage marker _____ .

4. A _____ state highway _____ crosses one state.

5. An area with many things in common is a _____ region _____ .

Map Check

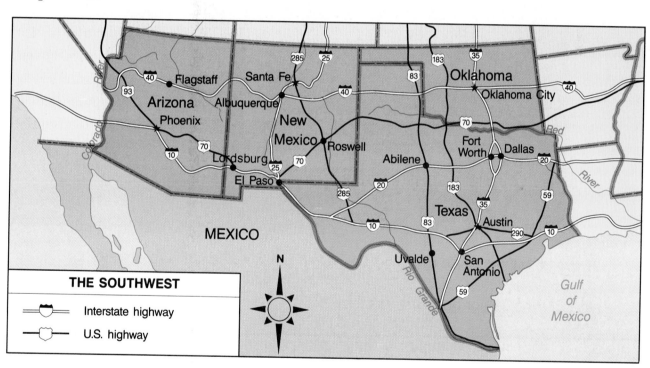

THE SOUTHWEST

Interstate highway

U.S. highway

1. What interstate highway splits to go through Dallas and Fort Worth? __I-35__

2. What route goes through the capital of Arizona? _____ I-10 _____

3. What route goes along part of the Red River? _____ U.S. 70 _____

4. What route goes through both the capital of Oklahoma and the capital
   of Texas? _____ I-35 _____

5. What interstate highways would you take from Flagstaff to Abilene via
   Albuquerque and El Paso? _____ I-40, I-25, I-10, I-20 _____

Geography Themes Up Close

Movement describes how people, goods, information, and ideas move from place to place. Movement shows people interacting. It demonstrates **interdependence**, or how people depend on one another, to meet their needs and wants. The St. Lawrence Seaway is a waterway that connects the Atlantic Ocean with the Great Lakes. This waterway lies in Canada and in the United States.

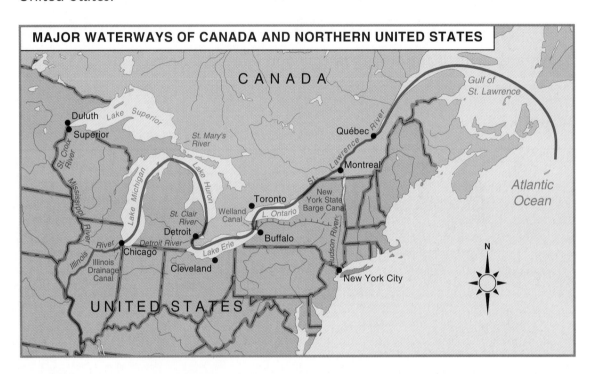

MAJOR WATERWAYS OF CANADA AND NORTHERN UNITED STATES

1. Trace the route of a ship that travels from the Atlantic Ocean into the Gulf of St. Lawrence, through the St. Lawrence Seaway, to the Mississippi River.

2. What major bodies of water does this ship pass through?

   Atlantic Ocean, Gulf of St. Lawrence, St. Lawrence River, Lake Ontario,

   Welland Canal, Lake Erie, Detroit River, St. Clair River, Lake Huron,

   Lake Michigan, Illinois Drainage Canal, Illinois River

3. What cities would the ship pass on its way to Chicago?

   Québec, Montreal, Toronto, Buffalo, Cleveland, Detroit

4. What major bodies of water would a ship pass through, traveling from Duluth to New York City?

Lake Superior, St. Mary's River, Lake Huron, St. Clair River, Detroit

River, Lake Erie, New York State Barge Canal, Hudson River

5. How do these waterways show interdependence and make the movement of people and goods easier between people in the United States and Canada?

Answers will vary, accept all reasonable answers. Students might point

out that the waterways connect a large portion of both countries

making transportation of goods and people possible.

Charts show facts in columns and rows. The chart below shows facts about using communication tools.

Use of Communication Tools in the United States

Number of hours per person per year			
	1995	2000	2005 (est.)
Television	1,575	1,633	1,679
Radio	1,091	961	998
Newspapers	165	151	144
Books	99	90	84
Magazines	84	107	100
Internet	7	124	194

6. According to the chart, which communication tool is most used by people in

the United States? television

7. Which communication tool is used the least in the United States? Why do you think this is so?

Internet. Answers will vary. Accept all reasonable answers. Students might point out

that fewer people have access to computers than to the other communication tools

shown in the chart, and that not all people who own computers use the Internet.

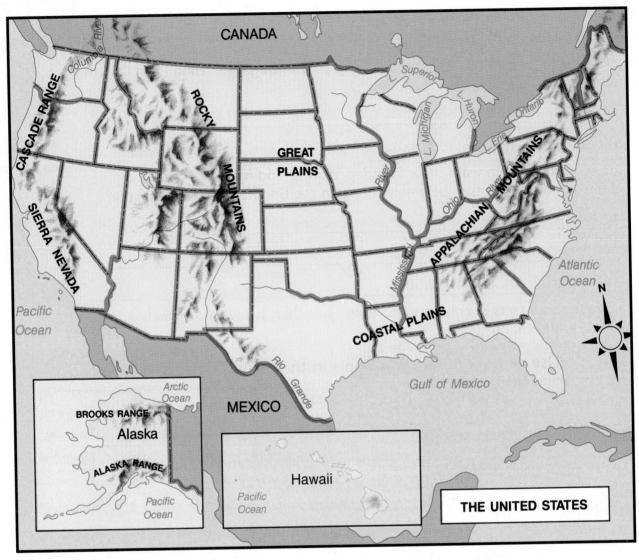

Maps have many purposes. Route maps show us how to get from one place to another. **Relief maps** show different landforms on Earth. Look at the relief map above. It shows the United States. You can see mountain ranges, plains, lakes, and rivers.

A **mountain range** is a group or chain of mountains. Find the Rocky Mountains on the map. A **plain** is a large area of level, treeless land. Now find the Great Plains. Which is darker, the mountains or the plains?   **mountains**

Relief maps help us picture how the land looks. The dark shading on relief maps stands for mountains. Higher mountains appear the darkest. Since plains are very flat, we do not see any shading.

Answers will vary according to state.

► Locate your own state. Is your state mostly mountains or plains?

► Name the mountain ranges and plains shown on the map.

► What is the highest mountain range on the map? How do you know?   **Rocky Mountains/ darkest shading**

► Are there more mountains in the eastern or in the western United States?   **western**

► Locate the inset map of Alaska. Are there more mountains or plains?   **plains**

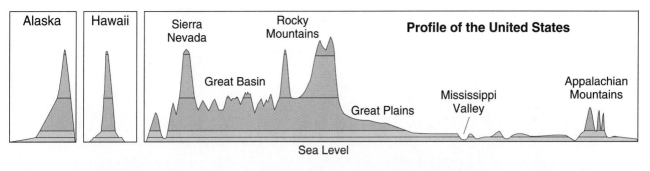

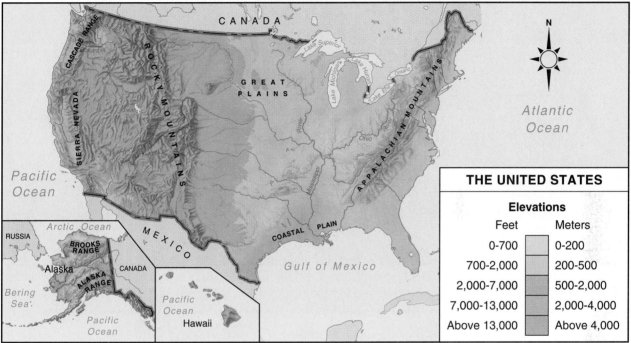

Sea level is the level of the ocean surface. Land that is even with the ocean is at sea level. Land that is higher than the ocean is above sea level. Elevation means the height of the land above sea level. Look at the diagram. It shows a side-view of the mountains, valleys, and plains of the United States. Each color in the legend and diagram stands for a different elevation. Elevation is measured in feet or meters.

A physical map combines elevation and relief. The physical maps above show the United States. The colors in the legend tell you the elevation of the land. This makes it easy to understand what the United States really looks like. Physical maps may also show cities, boundaries, mountain peaks, and rivers.

► On the map above, what color shows the elevation of the highest mountain peaks? blue

► What color is used to show the elevation of the Great Plains? light green

► Locate the area on the map where you live.
  What is the elevation of the area where you live? Answers will vary according to region.

► Find the Rocky Mountains in the diagram. What colors are used to show their elevation? Find the Rocky Mountains on the map. What colors are used to show their elevation? blue, purple, dark green; The map colors are the same as the diagram.

Physical Maps **37**

Reading a Physical Map

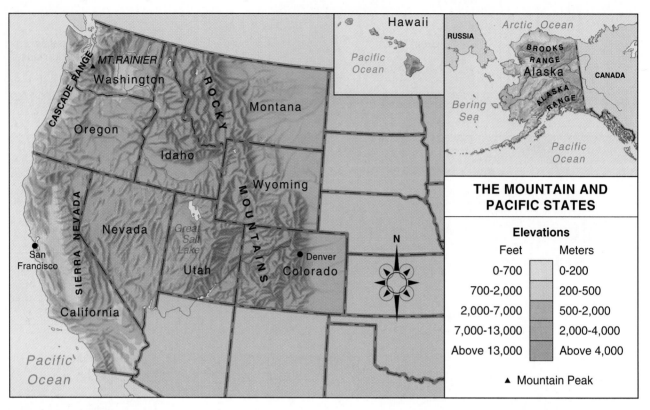

MAP ATTACK!

- **Read the title.** This map shows <u>the Mountain and Pacific States</u>.

- **Read the legend.** What color is land above 13,000 feet? <u>blue</u>
- **Read the compass rose.** Circle the intermediate direction arrows.

1. Which color in the legend stands for the lowest elevation? <u>yellow</u>

Complete each sentence below.

2. Find the Great Salt Lake in Utah. The elevation of this area is between 2,000 and 7,000 feet or between <u>500</u> and <u>2,000</u> meters.

3. Find Denver, Colorado. The elevation of this city is between <u>2,000</u> and <u>7,000</u> feet or between <u>500</u> and <u>2,000</u> meters.

4. Find San Francisco, California. The elevation of this city is between <u>0</u> and <u>700</u> feet or between <u>0</u> and <u>200</u> meters.

5. Find the symbol for mountain peak in the legend. What is the name of a mountain peak in the state of Washington? <u>Mt. Rainier</u>

Reading a Physical Map

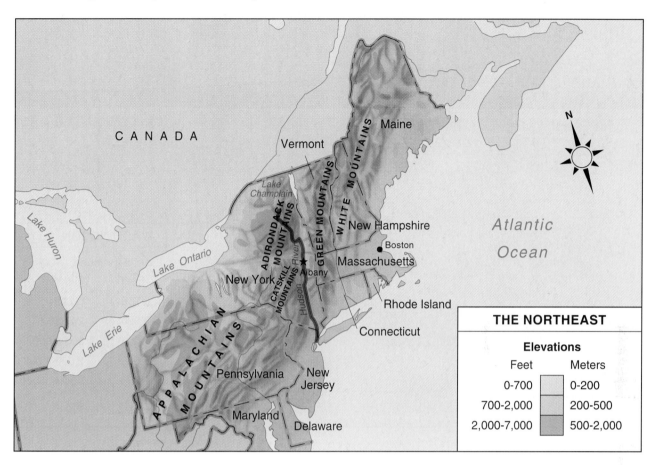

1. Look at the land along the coast of the Atlantic Ocean. Is this land mountainous or flat? _____ flat _____

2. Which state has only low elevation and is all the same color?

   _____ Rhode Island _____

3. Which are higher, the Catskill Mountains or the White Mountains?

   _____ the White Mountains _____

4. What lake lies near the northwestern edge of the Green Mountains?

   _____ Lake Champlain _____

5. Trace the Hudson River. The Hudson River flows into what body of

   water? _____ the Atlantic Ocean _____

6. The elevation of Boston is between ____0____ and ____700____ feet or

   between ____0____ and ____200____ meters.

7. Draw a conclusion. Would it be easy to hike from the White Mountains

   to Albany? Why or why not? Answers will vary but may include the following: Hikers would have several changes in elevation, which could be difficult. However, the overall elevation of the mountains is not that great.

Reading a Physical Map

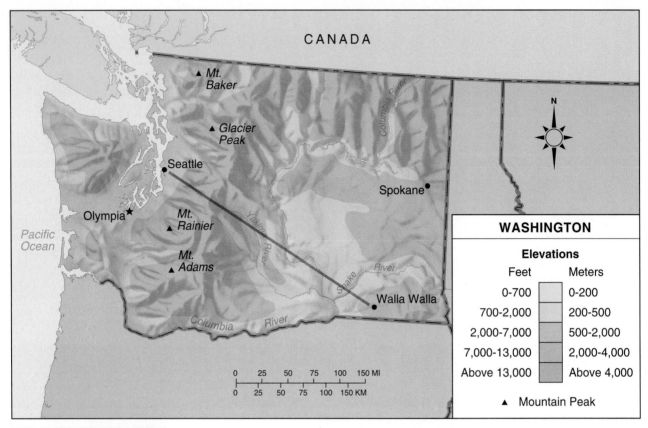

MAP ATTACK!

Follow the steps on page 38 to begin reading this map.

1. What is the state capital of Washington? _____ Olympia _____

2. The elevation of the state capital is between ___ 0 ___ and ___ 700 ___ feet.

3. What direction is Seattle from the state capital? ___ northeast ___

4. How many miles is it from the state capital to Seattle? Use a ruler and the map scale. The distance is about ___ 50 ___ miles.

5. From Seattle, which direction would you travel to reach an international border? ___ north ___

6. From Seattle, which direction would you travel to reach a boundary formed by a river? ___ south ___

7. Which is higher, Seattle or Spokane? ___ Spokane ___

8. Draw a conclusion. Draw a line from Walla Walla to Seattle. What problems would you face if you built a highway from Walla Walla to Seattle? ___ Answers will vary but may include the following: The road would cross rivers at several points and would cover several changes in elevation. ___

Skill Check

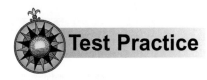

Vocabulary Check   relief map   plain   mountain range
                       physical map   elevation

1. The height of the land in feet or meters is called _____elevation_____.

2. A _____mountain range_____ is a group of mountains.

3. A _____relief map_____ shows the landforms on Earth.

4. A _____plain_____ is a large area of flat land.

5. A map that shows changes in elevation is called a _____physical map_____.

Map Check

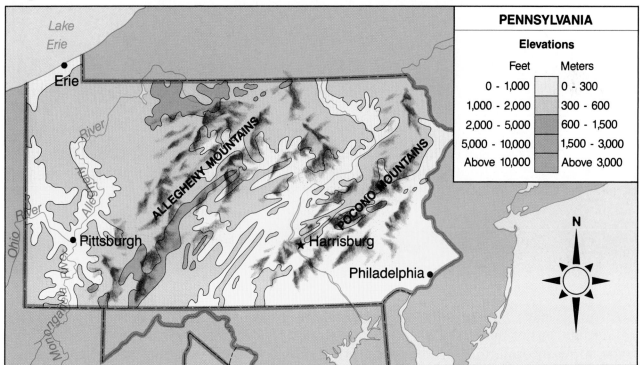

1. Which mountains are higher, the Allegheny Mountains or the Pocono
   Mountains? _____The Allegheny Mountains_____

2. What three rivers meet in Pittsburgh?
   _____Ohio, Monongahela, and Allegheny_____

3. Is Erie at a higher or lower elevation than Philadelphia? _____same_____

4. What is the state capital of Pennsylvania? _____Harrisburg_____

5. The elevation of the state capital is between ____0____ and ____1,000____
   feet or between ____0____ and ____300____ meters.

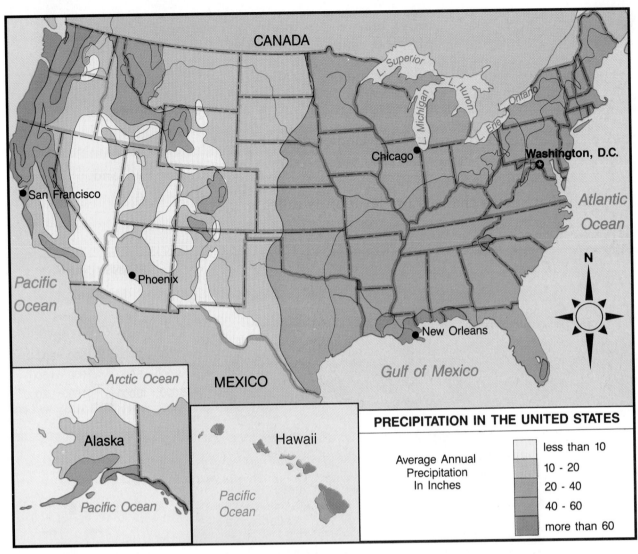

PRECIPITATION IN THE UNITED STATES

Average Annual
Precipitation
In Inches

	less than 10
	10 - 20
	20 - 40
	40 - 60
	more than 60

All maps have a purpose. Route maps show ways to get from one place to another. Relief maps show us how the land looks. **Special purpose** maps show information not found on other maps. The information may be about the climate, the people, the resources, or the history of an area. You need to read each map's title and legend carefully.

Use the map reading skills you've learned to read a special purpose map. Read the title carefully. The title tells you what the map shows. This map shows precipitation in the United States. Precipitation is rain and snow.

Read the legend carefully. The legend tells you what the symbols mean. On this map, colors are used as symbols. Remember that a **symbol** is something that stands for something else. Here each color stands for a different amount of precipitation.

► What color stands for 20-40 inches of precipitation per year? pink
What areas on the map get 20-40 inches of precipitation per year?
Pacific States, Mountain States, Great Lakes States, Plains States, Northeast
► Does more precipitation fall along the coastlines or inland? along coastlines

► Which areas of the United States get the most precipitation? Pacific States, Southeast

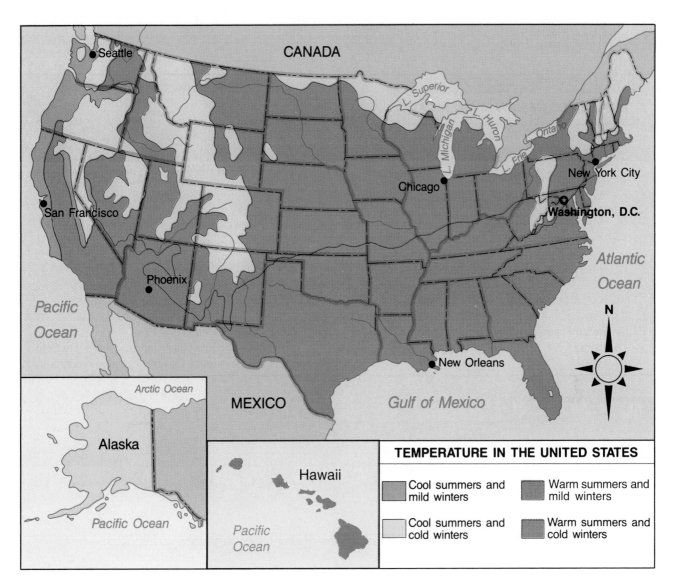

There are many types of special purpose maps. A **resource map** uses symbols for things in nature that people can use. In the legend you may find symbols for things like gold, oil, or coal. These symbols will appear on the map in the area where the resource is found.

Population maps show the number of people living in an area. The population of an area may be shown by using colors, dots of different sizes, or both.

Above is a **temperature map**. The legend shows summer and winter temperatures in the United States. It tells you that green areas have warm summers and cold winters. What color shows warm summers and mild winters? purple/blue

► What kind of temperatures does New York City have? warm summers and cold winters

► Look at the inset maps. What kind of temperatures do Alaska and Hawaii have? Alaska: cool summers, cold winters; Hawaii: warm summers, mild winters

► What kind of temperatures does Seattle have? cool summers, mild winters

► Locate your state on the map on page 42 and the map above. Describe the climate where you live. What kind of temperatures and how much precipitation does your state have? Answers will vary according to state.

Reading a Historical Map

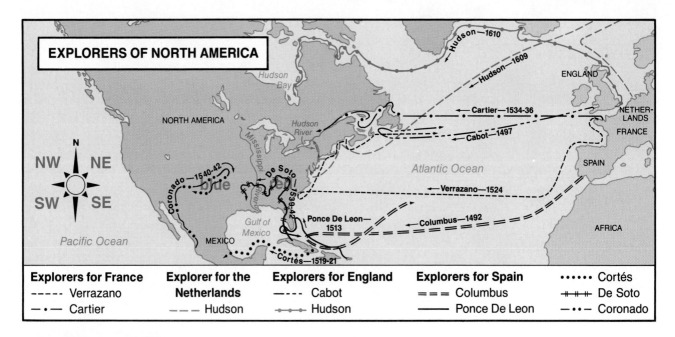

EXPLORERS OF NORTH AMERICA

Hudson—1610

Hudson—1609

ENGLAND

Cartier—1534-36

NETHER-LANDS

Cabot—1497

FRANCE

Hudson Bay

Hudson River

NORTH AMERICA

Mississippi River

Atlantic Ocean

SPAIN

Verrazano—1524

Coronado—1540-42

De Soto

1539-42

NW   NE

N

SW   SE

Ponce De Leon—1513

Columbus—1492

AFRICA

Gulf of Mexico

Pacific Ocean

MEXICO

Cortés—1519-21

Explorers for France	**Explorer for the Netherlands**	**Explorers for England**	**Explorers for Spain**	•••••• Cortés
----- Verrazano		—-- Cabot	=== Columbus	+++ De Soto
—•— Cartier	— — Hudson	+•+•+ Hudson	—— Ponce De Leon	—••— Coronado

MAP ATTACK!

- **Read the title.** This map shows ___Explorers of North America___.
- **Read the legend.** Check (✔) each symbol as you read its meaning.
- **Read the compass rose.** Label the intermediate direction arrows.

1. Find Columbus in the legend. What color shows his voyage? ___black___

2. In what country did Columbus start? ___Spain___

3. Which explorer made two trips to the New World? ___Hudson___

   a. Where did he begin his first voyage? ___the Netherlands___

   b. In what years were his voyages? ___1609 and 1610___

   c. What is a body of water named after this explorer?
   ___Hudson Bay or Hudson River___

4. Trace DeSoto's route in red.

   What river did he cross? ___Mississippi River___

5. Trace Coronado's route in blue.

   In what country did he start? ___Mexico___

6. DeSoto and Coronado were explorers for what country? ___Spain___

7. Draw a conclusion. Did most of the explorers for Spain travel to the

   northern or southern regions of North America? ___southern___

Reading a Population Map

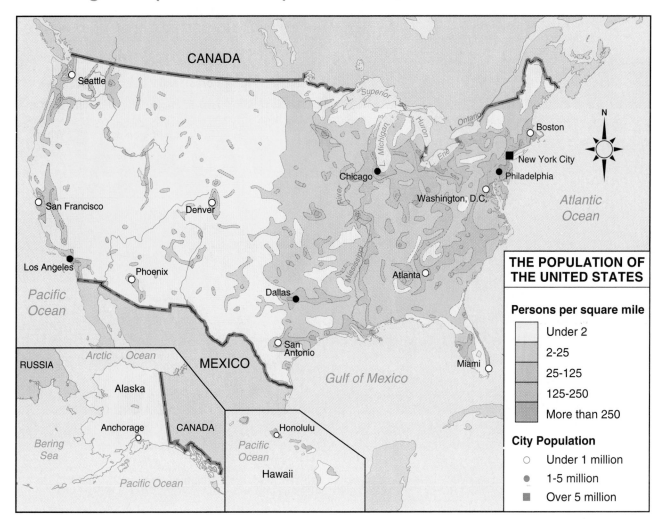

1. The purpose of this map is to show
   the population of the United States.

2. What color shows less than 2 people per square mile? ____yellow____

3. Do you find more of this color in the eastern or in the western United
   States? ____western____

4. What color shows more than 500 people per square mile? ___dark blue___

5. Add these symbols to the legend.   ○ City of under 1 million
                                       ● 1–5 million
                                       ■ Over 5 million

6. Name three cities that have 1 to 5 million people _Any three are correct:_
   Chicago,   _Philadelphia,_   and ___Los Angeles,___ _or Dallas_

7. What city has the largest population? ____New York City____

Reading a Land Use Map

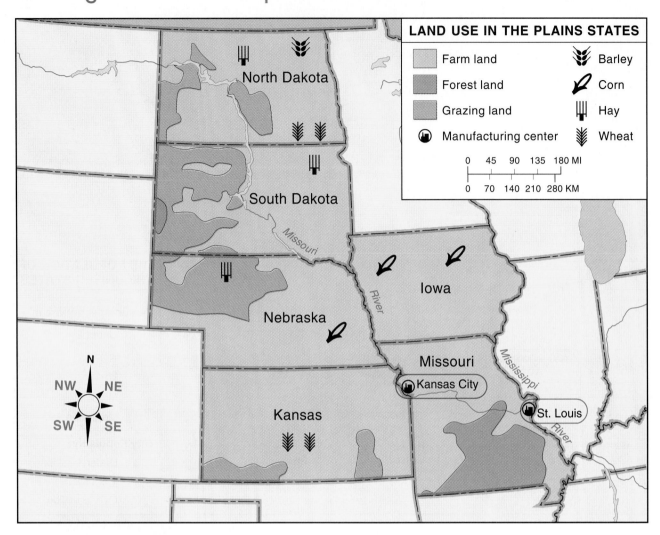

MAP ATTACK!

Follow the steps on page 44 to begin reading this map.

1. The purpose of this map is to show __land use in the Plains States__.

2. What is the most common use of land in these states? __farm land__

3. In which state is barley grown? __North Dakota__

4. In which states is corn grown? __Iowa and Nebraska__

5. What is the most common use of land in western South Dakota?

   __grazing land__

6. In what part of Kansas is there grazing land? __south__

7. There are two manufacturing centers in this region. Circle them.

   a. What are they? __Kansas City and St. Louis__

   b. About how far apart are they? __about 225 miles__

Skill Check

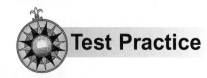

Test Practice

Vocabulary Check   **special purpose map   temperature map   symbol**
resource map   population map

Write the word that makes each sentence true.

1. A map showing the number of people in an area is a ___population map___.

2. A map showing special information is a ___special purpose map___.

3. A ___resource map___ shows things found in nature that people can use.

Map Check

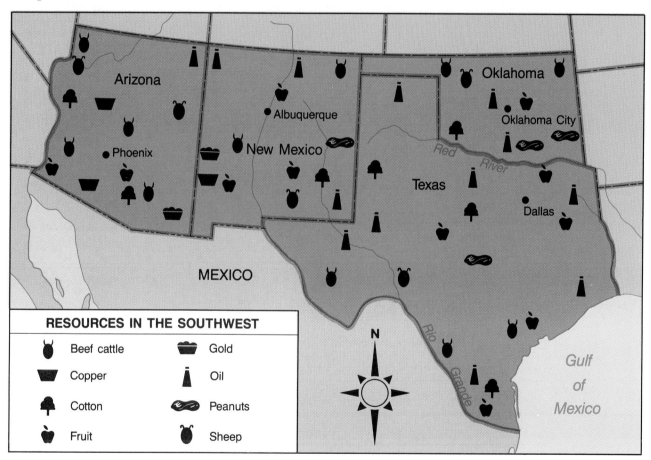

1. Gold is found in which states? ___Arizona and New Mexico___

2. Is there more oil in Arizona or in Texas? ___Texas___

3. Cotton can be found in every state on this map. Name two other
   resources that can be found in all four states. ___Beef cattle, sheep, fruit, or oil___

4. Which state does not grow peanuts? ___Arizona___

5. Copper is found in which two states? ___Arizona and New Mexico___

Geography Themes Up Close

Human/Environment Interaction shows how the environment and people affect one another. Sometimes people create problems. An example is pollution. One kind of pollution is **acid rain**—pollution that mixes with water vapor and falls to the ground in the form of rain or snow. This pollution comes from factories, power plants, and cars and trucks that burn coal, oil, and gas. Acid rain kills fish and destroys forests. It pollutes drinking water and soil and damages buildings. The map below shows recent acid rain levels in the United States and Canada.

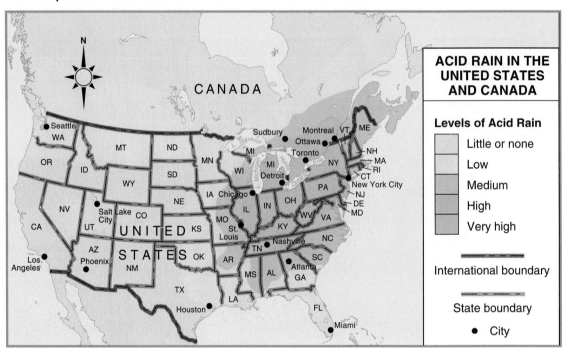

1. According to the map, where are the highest levels of acid rain found?

   near Montreal, Lake Ontario, Lake Huron, Lake Erie, Lake Michigan, in

   parts of Michigan, New York, Pennsylvania, West Virginia, Ohio,

   Indiana, Illinois, Kentucky, Chicago, Detroit, and Toronto

2. Describe acid rain levels in western Canada and the western United States.

   These areas have the least amounts of acid rain.

3. Based on the map, where do you think most manufacturing centers are located in the United States and Canada? Explain your answer.

   Answers will vary, but students might answer the northeastern United

   States and southeastern Canada, because acid rain levels are highest

   in these areas, and pollution from factories helps cause acid rain.

Human/Environment Interaction includes how people depend on the environment. The map shown here demonstrates how people in Mexico use the land and its resources to meet their needs and wants.

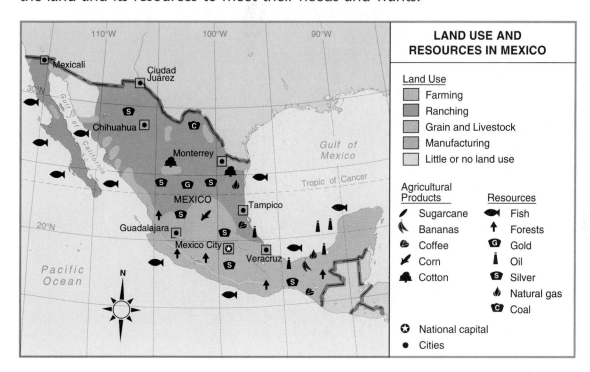

4. According to the map, where is fishing an important activity?

   all coastal areas of Mexico

5. Where is manufacturing an important activity?
   in the major cities: Mexico City, Guadalajara, Monterrey, Ciudad Juárez, Veracruz, Tampico, Chihuahua, Mexicali

6. Where is most of the farming done in Mexico?

   in southern and eastern Mexico

7. Based on the map key and map, where would you expect Mexico's population to be the smallest?

   in areas of little or no land use

8. Along which of these coasts would be a better location for oil refineries: Pacific Ocean, Gulf of Mexico, or Gulf of California? Why?

   Gulf of Mexico because of the oil there

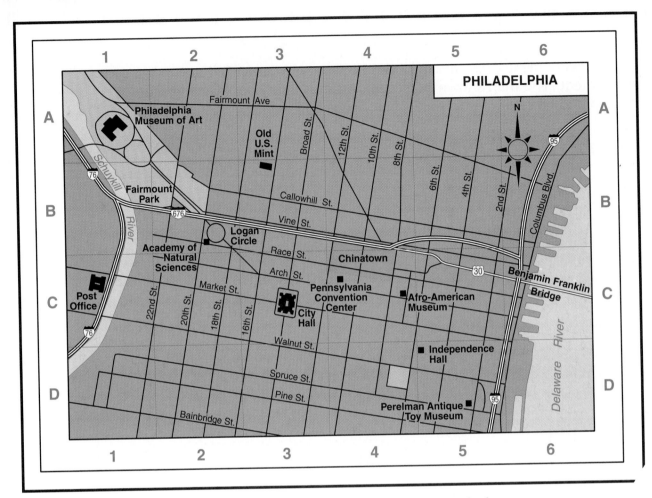

A **grid** is a pattern of lines drawn on a map to help people locate places. These lines form squares. Do you see the squares on the map above?

Now find the letters at each side of the map. The letters label the rows of squares. Numbers at the top and bottom label the columns of squares.

Locate City Hall on the map above. It is in square C-3. Find the letter C on the left side of the map. Slide your finger across row C until you reach column 3. You are now in square C-3. Put your finger on City Hall.

► Now move your finger one square to the east. **Chinatown, Afro-American** This is square C-4. Name two points of interest in C-4. **Museum**

► Find the Perelman Antique Toy Museum. It is in square D-5. Name another historic site in this square that you could visit. **Independence Hall**

► The Philadelphia Museum of Art is in square A-1. This museum is in what park? **Fairmount Park** Put your finger on the museum. Slide it southeast through the park. The park ends near Logan Circle. In what grid square is Logan Circle? **B-2**

► Locate the Benjamin Franklin Bridge in square C-6. What river does it cross? **Delaware River** Can you name the other grid squares that this river flows through? **B-6, D-6**

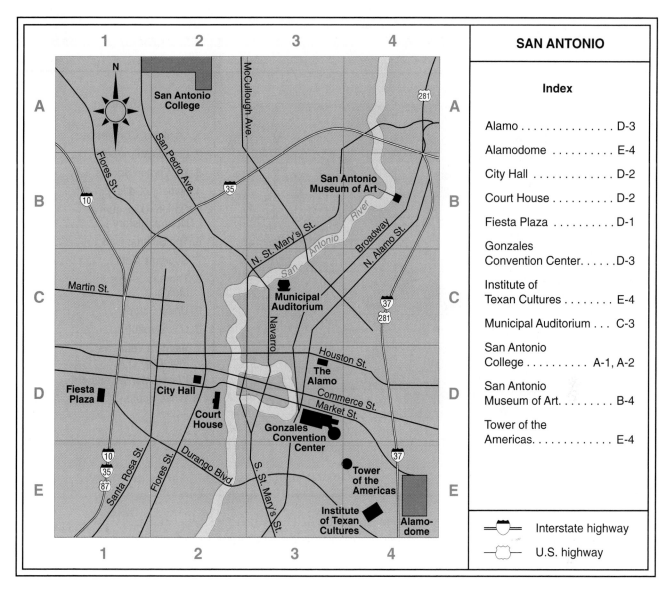

Index

Interstate highway

U.S. highway

To find a place on a map grid, you can look it up in the map index. A **map index** is an alphabetical list of all the places shown on the map. A map index lists each place with the letter and number of its grid square.

Look at the map above. It shows places of interest in San Antonio, Texas. To find places on the map, you use the map index. Imagine you want to visit the Alamo. Look up "Alamo" in the map index. It directs you to square D-3. Locate square D-3 on the grid. Do you see the Alamo?

▶ Use the map index to find City Hall. In what grid square is it located? **D-2**
  Find City Hall on the map. Name another point of interest in this square. **Court House**

▶ Look up the San Antonio Museum of Art in the map index.
  In what grid square is it located? **B-4**
  What direction is the San Antonio Museum of Art from City Hall? **northeast**

▶ Find San Antonio College by using the map index.
  In what grid squares is it located? **A-1, A-2**

▶ Locate the Institute of Texan Cultures using the map index.
  In what grid square is it located? **E-4**
  What other points of interest are located in this same square? **Tower of the Americas, Alamodome**

Reading a Map Grid

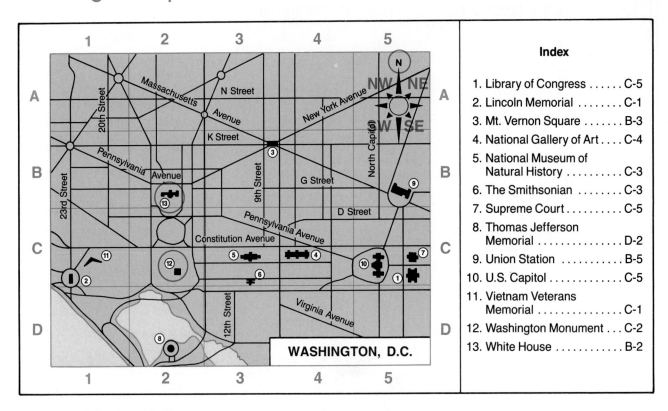

WASHINGTON, D.C.

MAP ATTACK!

● **Read the title.** This map shows _____Washington, D.C._____.
● **Read the compass rose.** Circle the north arrow. Label the
  intermediate directions.
● **Read the grid.** Add the missing letters and numbers.

Use the index and map to answer these questions.

1. In what square is the White House located? _____B-2_____
    Circle it on the map.

2. In what square is the Washington Monument? _____C-2_____
    Circle it on the map.
    What famous memorial is south of the Washington Monument?

    _____**Thomas Jefferson Memorial**_____

    What memorial is to the northwest? **Lincoln Memorial or Vietnam Veterans Memorial**

3. In what square is the U.S. Capitol located? _____C-5_____

    What two points of interest are to the east? _____

    _____**Supreme Court and Library of Congress**_____

Reading a Map Grid

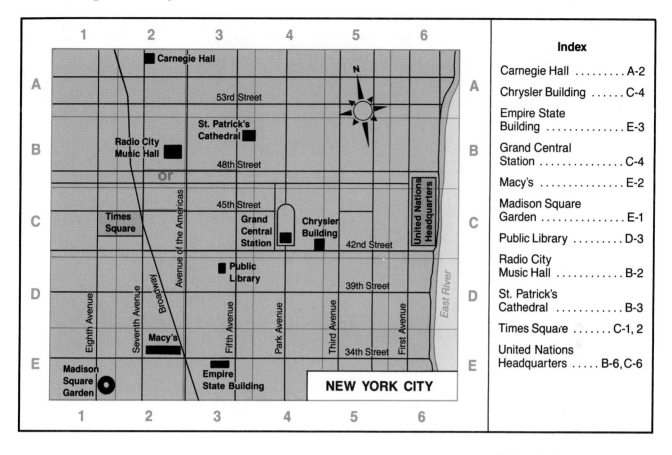

1. In what squares is the United Nations Headquarters located? __B-6, C-6__
   What avenue goes along the west side of the United Nations

   Headquarters? _____ First Avenue _____

2. In what grid squares is Times Square located? _____ C-1 and C-2 _____
   Draw a line along 42nd Street from the United Nations Headquarters
   to Times Square.
   Answers will vary but may include:
   Name one building you pass. _Chrysler Building, Grand Central Station, or Public Library._

3. In what grid square is Radio City Music Hall located? _____ B-2 _____
   Trace your route from Times Square to Radio City Music Hall.
   What avenue is just east of Radio City Music Hall?

   _____ Avenue of the Americas _____

4. In what grid square is the Empire State Building? _____ E-3 _____
   Trace your route from Radio City Music Hall east to Fifth Avenue.
   Trace your route to the Empire State Building.
   What street is just north of the Empire State Building?

   _____ 34th Street _____

Reading a Map Grid

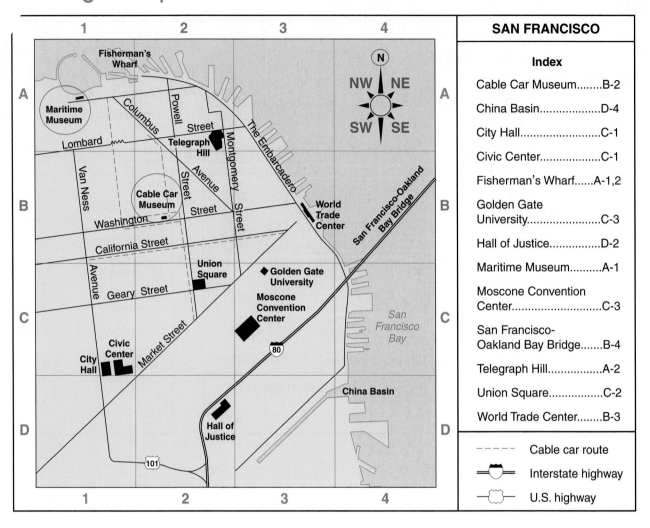

SAN FRANCISCO

Index

----- Cable car route

Interstate highway

U.S. highway

MAP ATTACK!

Follow the steps on page 52 to begin reading this map.

1. In what grid square do you find the Maritime Museum? _____**A-1**_____
   Circle it on the map.

2. In what grid square is the Cable Car Museum located? _____**B-2**_____
   Circle it on the map.

3. What direction is the Maritime Museum from the Cable Car Museum?

   _____**northwest**_____

4. Trace the cable car route from the Cable Car Museum to Union Square.

   Is Union Square east or west of the cable car route? _____**east**_____

5. What interstate highway is in San Francisco? _____**Interstate 80**_____

6. What U.S. highway is in San Francisco? _____**U.S. 101**_____

Skill Check

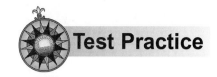

Vocabulary Check   grid   map index

1. A pattern of lines drawn on a map is called a _____ grid _____.

2. A _____ map index _____ is an alphabetized list of all the places shown on a map.

Map Check

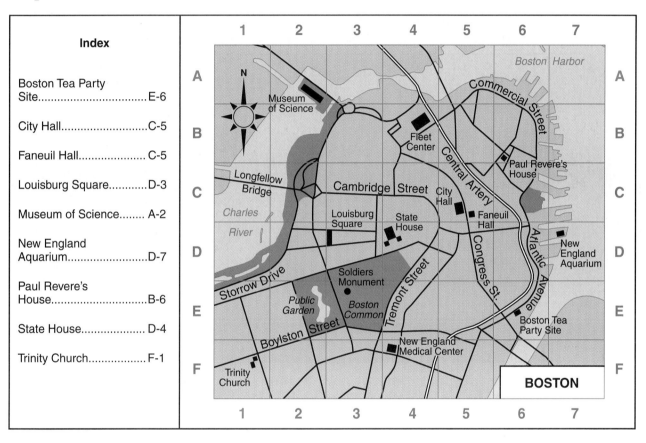

Index	
Boston Tea Party Site	E-6
City Hall	C-5
Faneuil Hall	C-5
Louisburg Square	D-3
Museum of Science	A-2
New England Aquarium	D-7
Paul Revere's House	B-6
State House	D-4
Trinity Church	F-1

1. Complete the grid by adding the missing letters and numbers.

2. In what grid square do you find City Hall? _____ C-5 _____
   Circle it.

3. In what grid square do you find Paul Revere's House? _____ B-6 _____
   What direction is Paul Revere's House from City Hall? _____ northeast _____

4. In what grid square is the New England Aquarium located? _____ D-7 _____
   What direction is the Aquarium from Paul Revere's House? _____ southeast _____

5. In what grid square is the Boston Tea Party Site located? _____ E-6 _____
   What direction is it from City Hall? _____ southeast _____

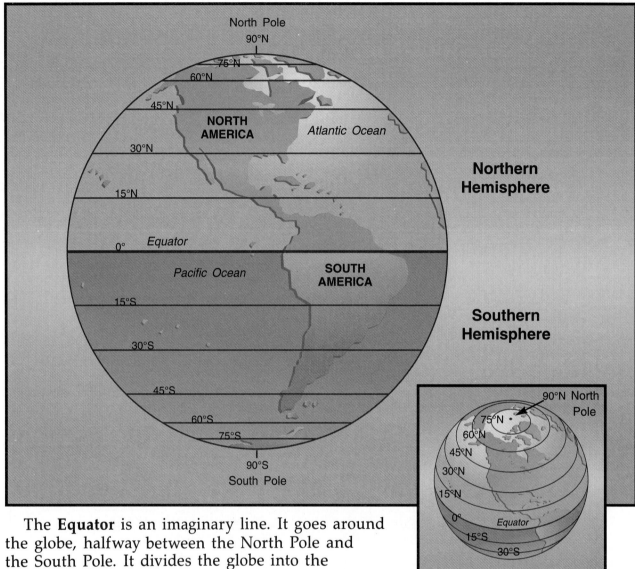

The **Equator** is an imaginary line. It goes around the globe, halfway between the North Pole and the South Pole. It divides the globe into the **Northern Hemisphere** and the **Southern Hemisphere**. Remember that the globe is a sphere. A **hemisphere** is half of a sphere.

The Equator is the most important line of **latitude**. The other lines of latitude measure distance on a globe north or south of the Equator. We use lines of latitude to locate places on the globe.

► Find the Equator on the large globe above.
  It is marked 0°. The symbol ° stands for **degrees**.

► Find the 45°N line of latitude. What continent does it cross? North America

► Find the 45°S line of latitude. What continent does it cross? South America

  Lines of latitude are also called **parallels**. Lines of latitude never touch.

► Look at the small globe above.
  Find the 75°N parallel.
  Does it touch any other parallel? no
  What continents does it cross? North America, Asia

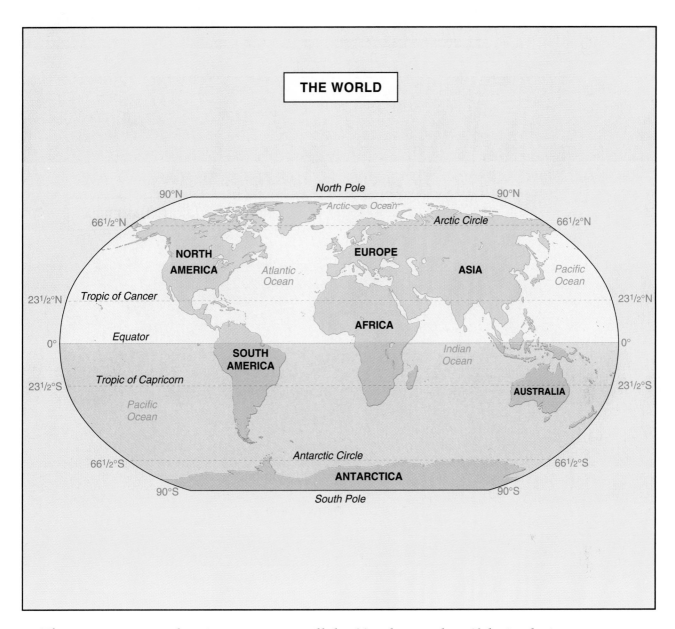

THE WORLD

There are some other important parallels. You know that 0° latitude is called the Equator. Other lines of latitude also have names. Find the line south of the Equator marked 23½°S. That line is called the **Tropic of Capricorn**.

Find the line north of the Equator marked 23½°N. That line is called the **Tropic of Cancer**.

Two other important lines of latitude are the **Arctic Circle** and the **Antarctic Circle**. The Arctic Circle is 66½°N of the Equator. Find the Arctic Circle on the map above. The Antarctic Circle is 66½°S of the Equator. Find the Antarctic Circle on the map above.

► The Tropic of Cancer goes through which continents? North America, Africa, Asia

► The Tropic of Capricorn goes through which oceans? Pacific, Atlantic, Indian

► The Arctic Circle goes through which continents? North America, Europe, Asia

► The Antarctic Circle goes around which continent? Antarctica

► Which important parallel do you live nearest? Answers will vary, depending on location.

Finding Latitude

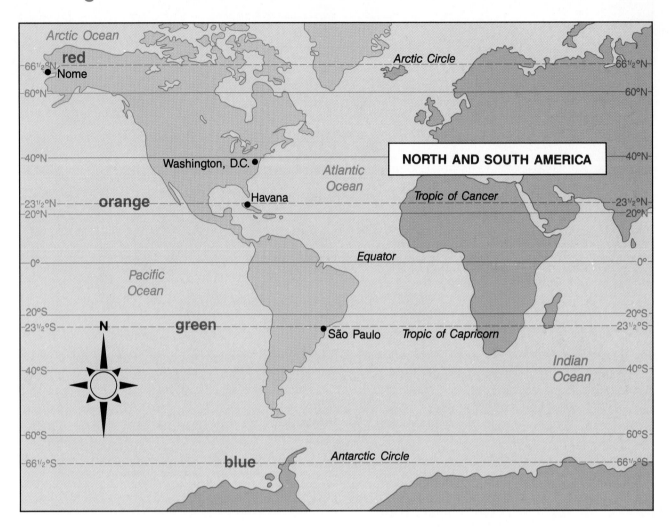

1. Trace the Arctic Circle in red.

   The Arctic Circle is in which hemisphere? _____ Northern Hemisphere _____

   What city lies near the Arctic Circle? _____ Nome _____

2. Trace the Antarctic Circle in blue.

   The Antarctic Circle is in which hemisphere? _____ Southern Hemisphere _____

   What oceans does the Antarctic Circle touch? _____ Atlantic, Pacific, and Indian _____

3. Trace the Tropic of Cancer in orange.

   The Tropic of Cancer is in which hemisphere? _____ Northern Hemisphere _____

   What city lies near the Tropic of Cancer? _____ Havana _____

4. Trace the Tropic of Capricorn in green. The Tropic of Capricorn

   is in which hemisphere? _____ Southern Hemisphere _____

   What city lies near the Tropic of Capricorn? _____ São Paulo _____

Finding Latitude

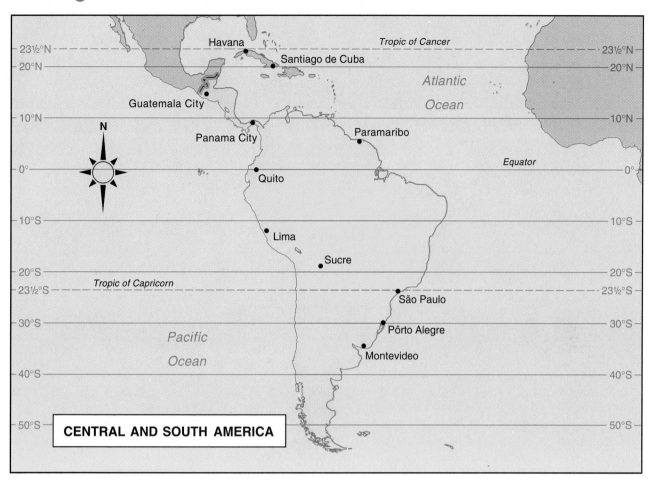

1. What city lies on the Equator? ___Quito___

2. What city lies near the Tropic of Cancer? ___Havana___

3. What city lies near the Tropic of Capricorn? ___São Paulo___

4. What city lies near 20°N? ___Santiago de Cuba___

5. What city lies near 10°N? ___Panama City___

6. What city lies near 20°S? ___Sucre___

7. What city lies at 30°S? ___Pôrto Alegre___

8. Guatemala City lies between 20°N and 10°N.

   Estimate its latitude. ___15°N or 16°N___

9. Paramaribo lies between 10°N and the Equator.

   Estimate its latitude. ___5°N or 6°N___

10. Montevideo lies between 30°S and 40°S.

    Estimate its latitude. ___34°S or 35°S___

Finding Latitude

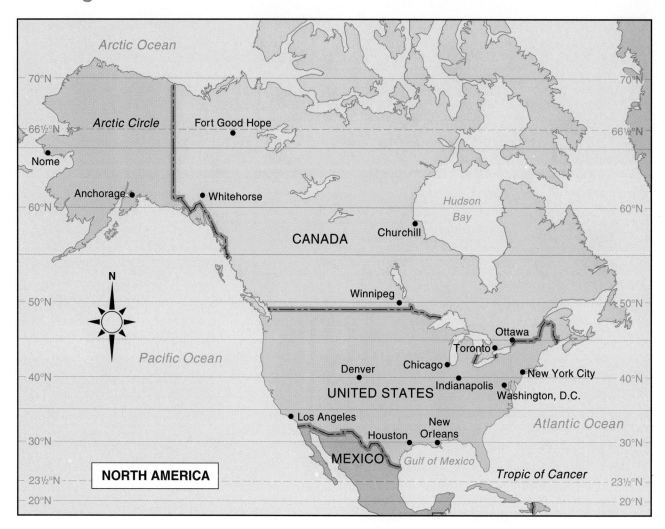

1. What two cities lie at 30°N? _____ New Orleans and Houston _____

2. What two cities lie at 40°N? _____ Denver and Indianapolis _____

3. What city lies at 50°N? _____ Winnipeg _____

4. What is another name for 66½°N latitude? _____ the Arctic Circle _____

5. What city lies near the Arctic Circle? _____ Fort Good Hope _____

6. Find Ottawa. It lies between 40°N and 50°N.

   Estimate its latitude. _____ 45°N _____

7. Find Los Angeles. It lies between 30°N and 40°N.

   Estimate its latitude. _____ 34°N or 35°N _____

8. What border runs along the 49°N line of latitude?

   _____ the U.S.-Canada border _____

9. Is Canada north or south of the Tropic of Cancer? _____ north _____

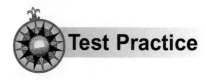

Test Practice

Vocabulary Check

Equator	latitude	parallcl
Tropic of Capricorn	Tropic of Cancer	degrees
Arctic Circle	Antarctic Circle	
Northern Hemisphere	Southern Hemisphere	

1. Another name for a line of latitude is a _____ parallel _____.

2. Latitude is measured in _____ degrees _____.

Map Check

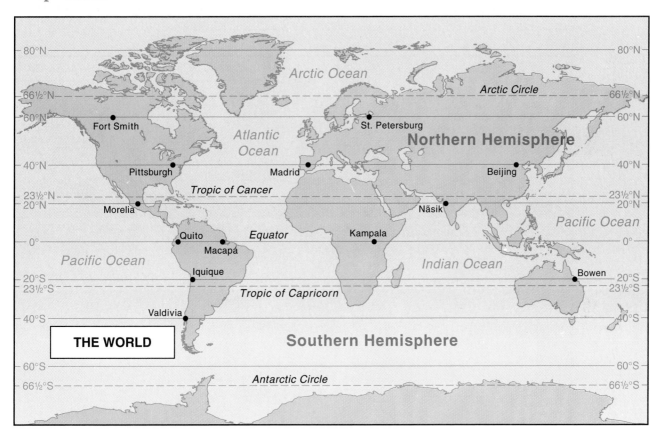

1. Label the Northern Hemisphere and the Southern Hemisphere on the map above.

2. What is another name for 66½°S latitude? _____ Antarctic Circle _____

3. What is another name for 23½°N latitude? _____ Tropic of Cancer _____

4. What two cities lie at 60°N? _____ Fort Smith and St. Petersburg _____

5. What two cities lie at 20°S? _____ Iquique and Bowen _____

6. What two cities lie at 20°N? _____ Morelia and Nāsik _____

7. What is the latitude of Quito? _____ 0° _____

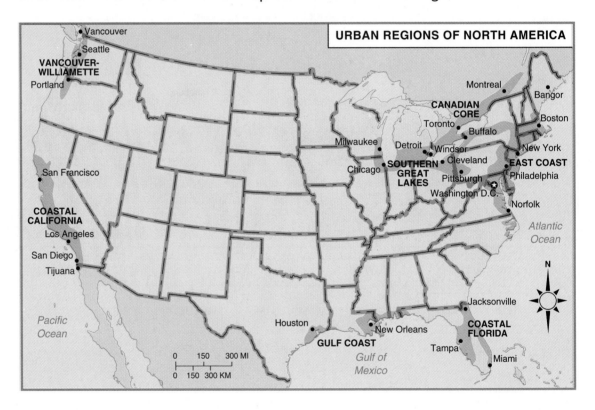

Geography Themes Up Close

Regions describes places that share one or more features. A region can be called physical because it is marked by a physical feature, such as climate. The Great Plains is a physical region of the United States that has grasslands as its common feature. A region can be called a human region if it is marked by a human feature, such as language.

The map shows the major urban centers in the United States and Canada. Each center is made up of several large cities and their suburbs that have increased in size and grown together. You can hardly tell where one city begins and another ends. Each urban center on the map can be considered a region.

1. What is similar about the location of each urban region in North America?

   Each is located along or near water.

2. Use a ruler and the map scale. How many miles long is the Coastal California urban region?

   about 700 miles

3. What cities make up the Vancouver-Willamette urban region?

   Vancouver, Seattle, Portland

Regions can be as large as a hemisphere or as small as a neighborhood. The map shows neighborhoods in New Orleans that can be considered regions.

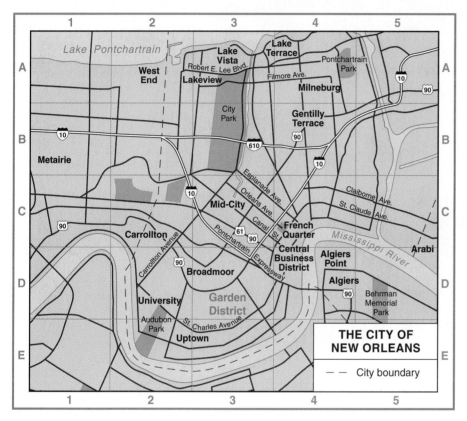

4. The Garden District is found in grid square D-3. This region has many old mansions and beautiful gardens. Label Garden District on the map.

5. What feature do you think the neighborhood called Lakeview has in common?

   The neighborhood has a view of Lake Pontchartrain.

6. What special features would you expect to find in the French Quarter?

   Answers will vary, but students might mention that French culture or

   style would be found there in homes and buildings, in food, and so on.

7. How could these neighborhood regions help the government of New Orleans organize the city?

   Answers will vary, but students may point out that these regions could

   be used as fire districts, police districts, school districts, or local

   government districts.

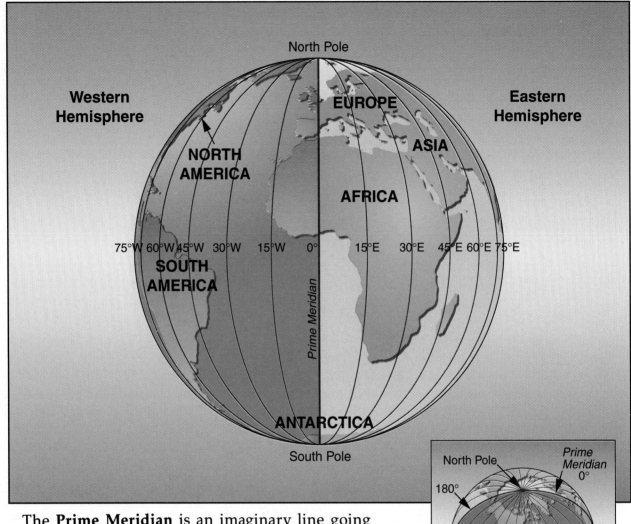

The **Prime Meridian** is an imaginary line going from the North Pole to the South Pole. The Prime Meridian is a line of **longitude**. It is marked 0°. The other lines of longitude measure distance on a globe east and west of the Prime Meridian. All lines of longitude meet at the North and South Poles. Lines of longitude are also called **meridians**.

The 180° meridian and the Prime Meridian form a circle around the globe. That circle divides the globe into two hemispheres. The hemisphere east of the Prime Meridian is the **Eastern Hemisphere**. The hemisphere west of the Prime Meridian is the **Western Hemisphere**.

► Find the Prime Meridian on the large globe above. What continents does it cross? Europe, Africa, Antarctica

► What continents and oceans are in the Eastern Hemisphere? Europe, Africa, Asia, Antarctica, Arctic, Atlantic, Pacific, Indian

► What continents and oceans are in the Western Hemisphere? North America, South America, Antarctica, Arctic, Atlantic, Pacific

► Find the 45°West meridian. What continents does it cross? South America, Antarctica

► Find the 45°East meridian. What continents does it cross? Africa, Asia, Europe, Antarctica

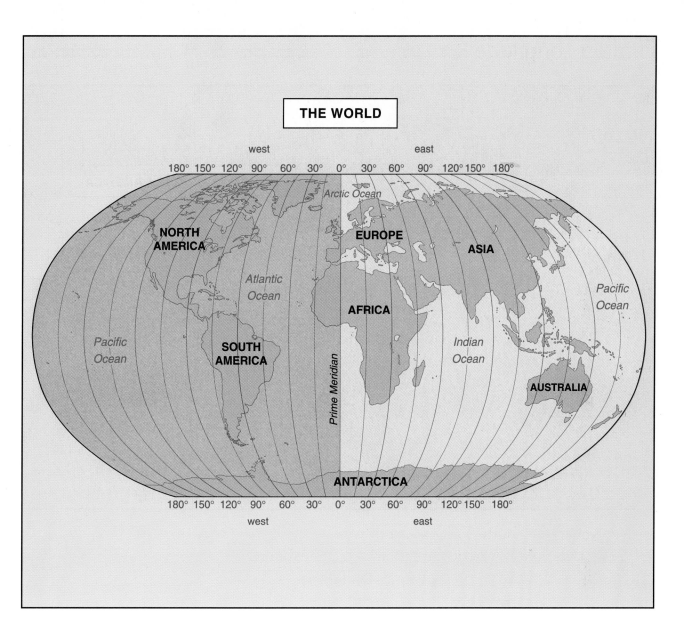

THE WORLD

Lines of longitude are measured in degrees. The Prime Meridian is 0°. All other meridians are numbered east and west of the Prime Meridian up to 180°. The meridians in the Eastern Hemisphere are marked with an E. The meridians in the Western Hemisphere are marked with a W.

► Find the Prime Meridian on the map.
  What oceans does it cross? **Arctic, Atlantic**

► Find the 180° meridian on each side of the map.
  Even though you see it twice, it is really the same line.
  What oceans does the 180° meridian cross? **Pacific, Arctic**

► Find the 30°E meridian.
  What continents does the 30°E meridian cross? **Europe, Africa, Antarctica**

► Find the 60°W meridian.
  What continents does the 60°W meridian cross? **North America, South America, Antarctica**

► Why do the meridians curve? **Earth is round. The curved lines show the spherical shape on a flat surface.**

Finding Longitude

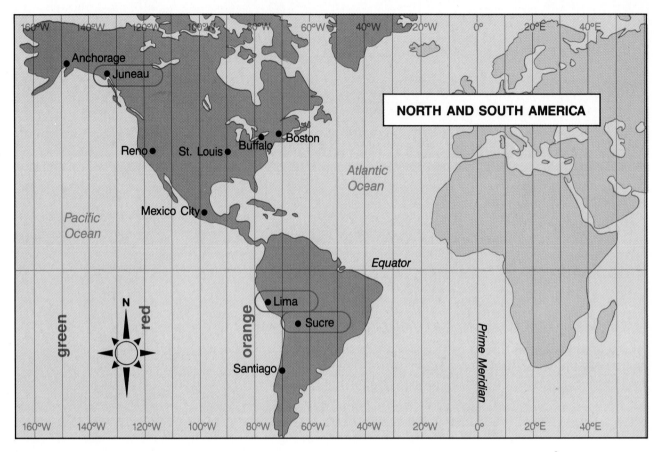

1. Are North and South America east or west of the Prime Meridian? __west__

2. North and South America are in which hemisphere?

   __Western Hemisphere__

3. Trace the 150°W meridian in green.

   What city is near 150°W? __Anchorage__

4. Trace the 120°W meridian in red.

   What city is near 120°W? __Reno__

5. Trace the 80°W meridian in orange.

   What city is nearest 80°W? __Buffalo__

6. Find Lima in South America. Circle it.

   Estimate the longitude of Lima. __75°W__

7. Find Sucre in South America. Circle it.

   Estimate the longitude of Sucre. __65°W__

8. Find Juneau in North America. Circle it.

   Estimate the longitude of Juneau. __135°W__

9. What city is north of the Equator and near 70°W longitude? __Boston__

Finding Longitude

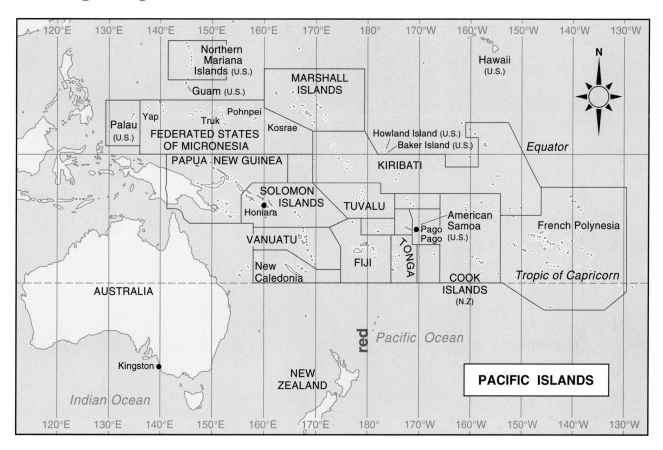

1. Trace the 180° meridian in red.
2. Are the Northern Mariana Islands in the Eastern Hemisphere or Western Hemisphere? _____**Eastern Hemisphere**_____
3. Is American Samoa in the Eastern Hemisphere or Western Hemisphere?
   _____**Western Hemisphere**_____
4. What city is at 160°E? _____**Honiara**_____
5. In the Federated States of Micronesia, what island is at 138°E? _____**Yap**_____
6. What U.S. island lies between 120°E and 140°E? _____**Palau**_____
7. What is the longitude of Kingston, Australia? _____**140°E**_____
8. Estimate the longitude of Pago Pago. _____**170°W**_____
9. Estimate the longitude of Guam. _____**144°E or 145°E**_____
10. Estimate the longitude of Hawaii. _____**155°W**_____
11. What two islands are just north of the Equator and at about 176°W?
    _____**Howland Island and Baker Island**_____

Finding Latitude and Longitude

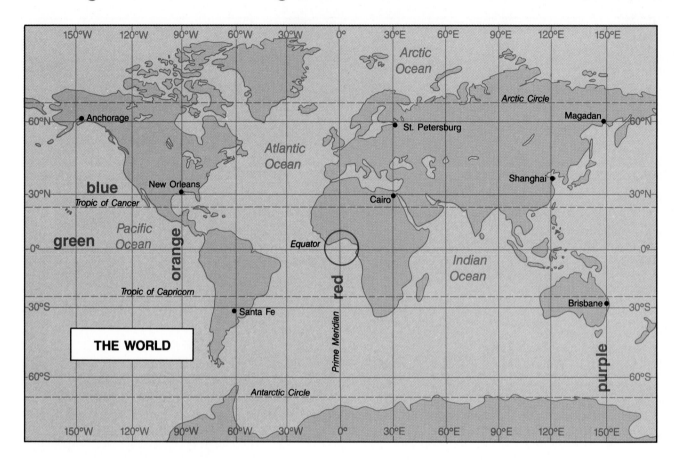

1. Trace the Equator in green.
2. Trace the Prime Meridian in red.
3. Circle the point where the Equator and the Prime Meridian cross.

   Is that point on land or on water? _____ **water** _____
4. Trace the 30°N latitude line in blue.
5. Trace the 90°W longitude line in orange.

6. What city is near the point where 30°N and 90°W cross? ___ **New Orleans** ___
7. Trace the 150°E longitude line in purple.
   What two cities lie near this line?

   a. ___ **Magadan 60°N** ___   b. ___ **Brisbane 28°S or 29°S** ___
8. To locate these cities, you also need to know their degrees latitude.
   Write their degrees latitude after their names in number 7.
9. Anchorage and St. Petersburg are near the same line of latitude.

   What is the line of latitude? ___ **60°N** ___
10. Anchorage and St. Petersburg are on different lines of longitude. Estimate
    their degrees longitude.

    Anchorage **148°W or 149°W** St. Petersburg **30°E or 31°E**

Skill Check

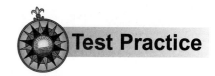

Vocabulary Check
    Prime Meridian   longitude   meridian
    Eastern Hemisphere   Western Hemisphere

1. Another word for a line of longitude is a _____ *meridian* _____.

2. The 0° longitude line is also called the _____ *Prime Meridian* _____.

3. The Prime Meridian and the 180° meridian divide the globe into the

   _____ *Eastern Hemisphere* _____ and the _____ *Western Hemisphere* _____.

Map Check

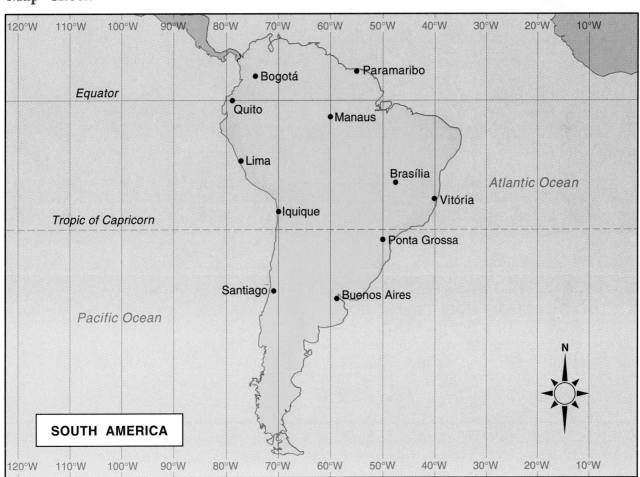

1. Is South America in the Eastern Hemisphere or the Western Hemisphere?

   _____ *Western Hemisphere* _____

2. What city lies at 40°W? _____ *Vitória* _____

3. Estimate the longitude of Paramaribo. _____ *55°W* _____

4. What city is south of the Tropic of Capricorn and near 70°W longitude?

   _____ *Santiago* _____

10 The Earth and the Sun

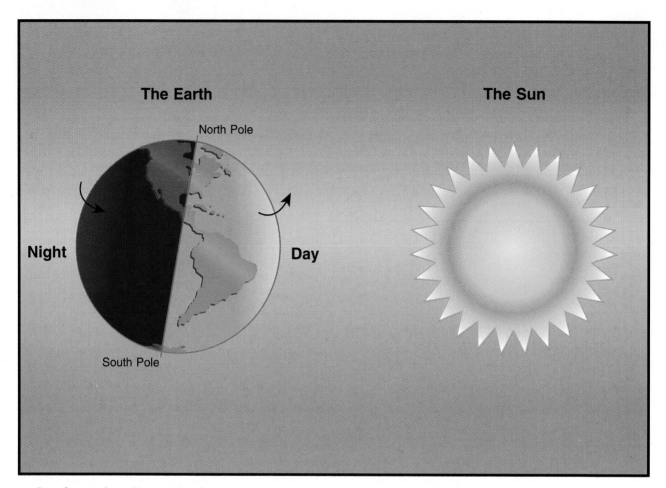

The Earth   The Sun

North Pole

Night   Day

South Pole

Look at the diagram above. It shows the Earth in relation to the sun. Our light comes from the sun.

An imaginary line goes through the Earth from the North Pole to the South Pole. This line is called the Earth's **axis**. Earth spins on its axis. This movement is called **rotation**. As the Earth rotates, the sun shines on part of it, making daylight. The other part of the Earth gets no sunlight, leaving it in the darkness of night.

Half of the Earth receives sunlight at a time. The opposite half of the Earth is in darkness. When it is daytime in North America, it is nighttime in India. When it is daytime along the Prime Meridian, it is nighttime along the 180° line of longitude, which is opposite the Prime Meridian.

Notice that the Earth is tilted. Areas along the Equator always get about the same amount of sunshine, winter or summer. At the North and South Poles, the amount of sunshine changes with the seasons. For a short time during the year, one pole gets sunshine all 24 hours every day. During this same time, the other pole gets no sunshine.

► If it is day in Europe, is it night or day in Australia? **day**

► If it is day in one place on the Equator, is it day everywhere else on the Equator? **no**

► Who sees the sun first, people in New York or people in California? **people in New York**

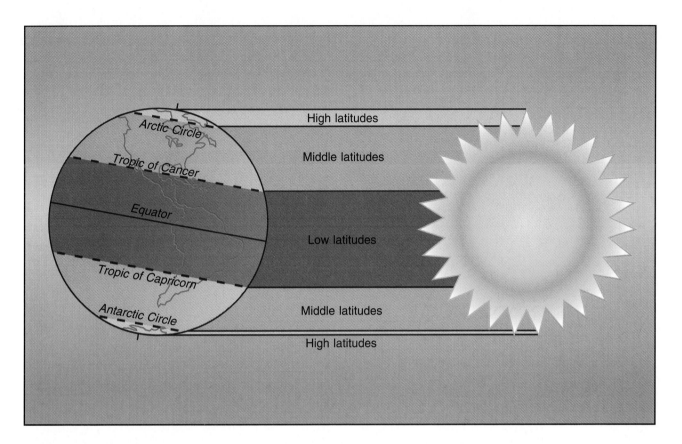

Because the Earth is round, the sun's rays reach the Earth in different ways. The rays are strongest and most direct at the Equator. But at the poles the rays are less strong and direct. Because of this, the Earth is divided into three **climate zones**. **Climate** is the average weather of one place over a long period of time.

Look at the diagram. The area between the Tropic of Capricorn and the Tropic of Cancer receives most of the sun's heat. This climate zone is called the **low latitudes**. Remember that the Equator is 0°. The latitudes close to the Equator have low latitude numbers. Generally the low latitudes have a warm climate.

Look at the areas near the North Pole and the South Pole. These areas receive the least of the sun's heat. They are called the **high latitudes**. The high latitudes are north of the Arctic Circle and south of the Antarctic Circle. Remember that the North and South Poles have the highest latitude numbers—90°. The climate of the high latitudes is usually cold.

Between the high and low latitudes are the **middle latitudes**. The middle latitudes fall between the Tropic of Cancer and the Arctic Circle, and between the Tropic of Capricorn and the Antarctic Circle. The middle latitudes are usually warm in summer and cool in winter.

▶ Find the high latitudes on the diagram.
  What continents are in the high latitudes? **North America, Antarctica**

▶ Find the middle latitudes on the diagram.
  What continents are in the middle latitudes? **North America, South America**

▶ Find the low latitudes on the diagram.
  What continents are in the low latitudes? **North America, South America**

Locating Temperature Zones

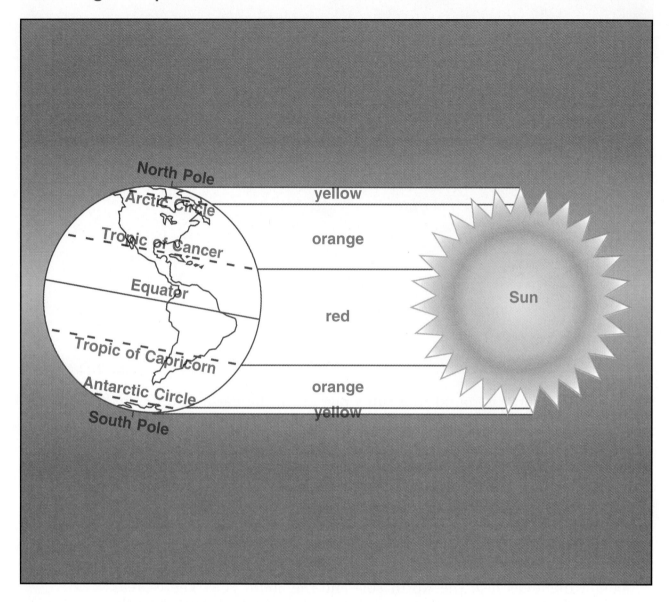

Finish this diagram.
1. Label the sun.
2. Label the Equator.
3. Label the Tropic of Cancer and the Tropic of Capricorn.
4. Label the Arctic Circle and the Antarctic Circle.
5. Label the North Pole and the South Pole.
6. Color the low latitudes red.
7. Color the middle latitudes orange.
8. Color the high latitudes yellow.

9. The North and South Poles are in which climate zone? __high latitudes__

10. The Equator is in which climate zone? __low latitudes__

Locating Temperature Zones

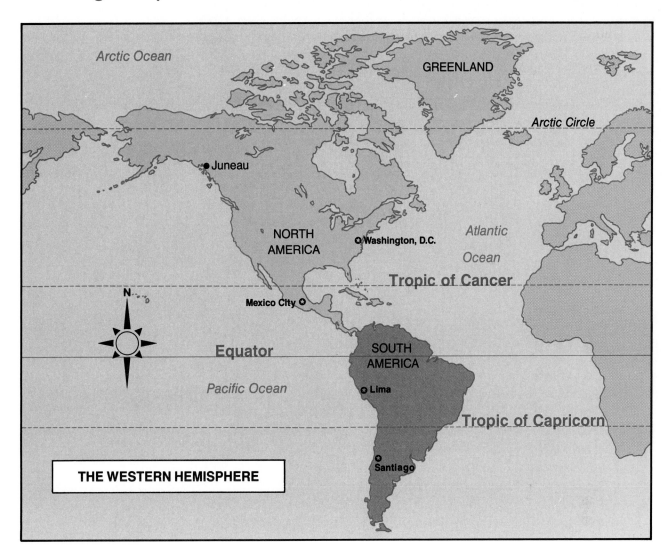

THE WESTERN HEMISPHERE

1. Label the Equator.
2. Label the Tropic of Cancer and the Tropic of Capricorn.

3. Greenland is mostly in what climate zone? _____ high latitudes _____

4. North America is in what three climate zones? _____ low latitudes _____

_____ middle latitudes _____ and _____ high latitudes _____

5. Most of North America is in which climate zone? _____ middle latitudes _____

6. Name two cities in the low latitudes. _____ Mexico City and Lima _____

7. Draw a conclusion. Do you think the climate would be warmer in the northern part of South America or in the southern part of South

America? _____ the northern part of South America _____

Why? _____ It is in the low latitudes. It is closer to the Equator. _____

Reading a Climate Map

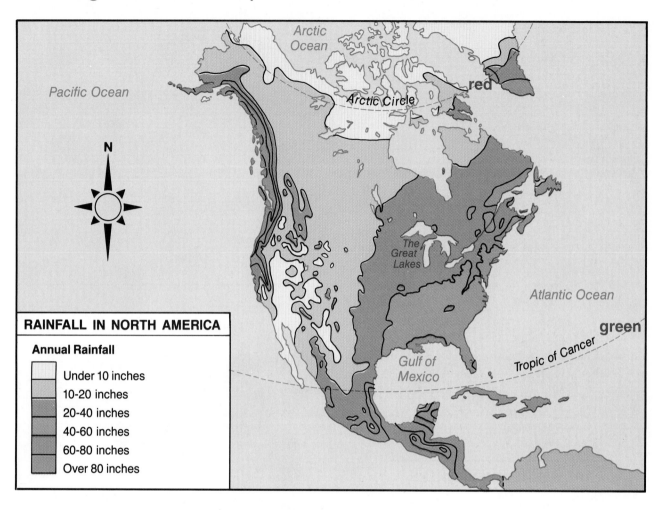

RAINFALL IN NORTH AMERICA

Annual Rainfall

- Under 10 inches
- 10-20 inches
- 20-40 inches
- 40-60 inches
- 60-80 inches
- Over 80 inches

1. Trace the Tropic of Cancer in green.

2. Is there more rain north or south of the Tropic of Cancer? _____ **south** _____

3. What climate zone is just south of the Tropic of Cancer? **low latitudes**

4. Would the weather there be warm and rainy or cold and rainy?

   _____ **warm and rainy** _____

5. Trace the Arctic Circle in red.

6. Is there more rain north or south of the Arctic Circle? _____ **south** _____

7. What climate zone is north of the Arctic Circle? _____ **high latitudes** _____

8. Would the weather there be cold and wet or cold and dry?

   _____ **cold and dry** _____

9. Draw a conclusion. Which latitudes in North America would be better

   for growing food, the high latitudes or the low latitudes? **low latitudes**

   Why? __**Answers will vary but may include: High latitudes are too cold and dry for growing food.**__

Skill Check

Test Practice

Vocabulary Check   axis   rotation   middle latitudes   climate zone
climate   low latitudes   high latitudes

1. The average weather of one place over a long period of time is called
   _____ climate _____.

2. The Earth spins on its _____ axis _____.

3. The climate zone south of the Antarctic Circle is called the
   _____ high latitudes _____.

4. The climate zone between the Tropic of Cancer and the Tropic of
   Capricorn is called the _____ low latitudes _____.

5. The climate zone between the Tropic of Cancer and the Arctic Circle
   is called the _____ middle latitudes _____.

Map Check

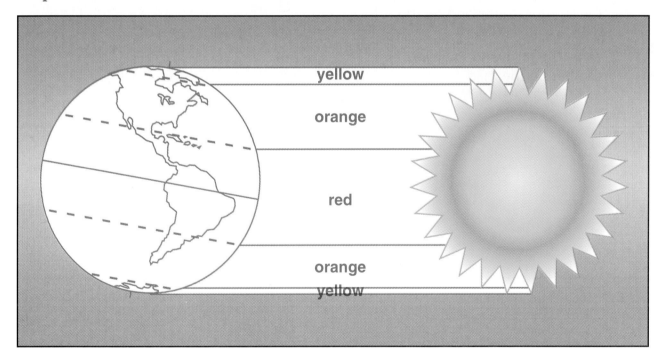

1. Color the high latitudes yellow.
2. Color the middle latitudes orange.
3. Color the low latitudes red.

4. North America is mostly in the _____ middle latitudes _____.

5. The Equator is in the _____ low latitudes _____.

6. Which climate zone has the coldest weather? _____ high latitudes _____

Geography Themes Up Close

Location tells where something is found. Every place on Earth has a location. There are two ways of naming a location. **Relative location** tells what it is near or what is around it. **Absolute location** gives the exact location by using latitude and longitude lines.

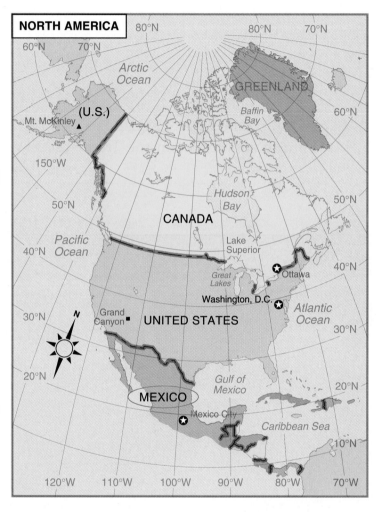

1. Greenland, the largest island in the world, is located northeast of Canada. Greenland is located east of Baffin Bay. Most of Greenland is north of the Arctic Circle. Label Greenland on the map.

2. Label the following national capitals on the map.
   a. Mexico City 19°N, 99°W
   b. Ottawa 45°N, 76°W

3. Label the following on the map.
   a. Mt. McKinley 63°N, 151°W
   b. Grand Canyon 36°N, 112°W
   c. Lake Superior 48°N, 89°W

4. Find Mexico on the map. Circle it. Describe the relative location of Mexico.

South of the United States, between the Pacific Ocean and the Gulf of

Mexico

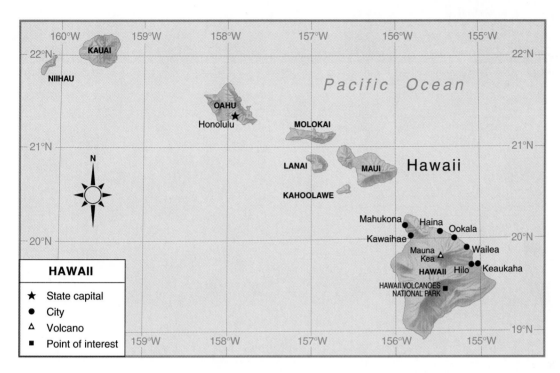

5. Describe the relative location of Honolulu. Explain why its location might be one reason Honolulu was chosen as the capital of Hawaii.

   It is on the middle island, which would make its location as the capital

   central to the rest of the islands.

6. What is the absolute location of the volcano Mauna Kea—the highest point in Hawaii?

   20°N, 155°W

7. Where are most cities and towns on the island of Hawaii located? Why do you think this is so?

   Near the ocean, along the coast. Answers will vary, but students might

   point out that the coast gives easy access to water travel, fish and

   seafood offer a food source, and that inland Hawaii is rugged and made

   up mostly of volcanic mountains.

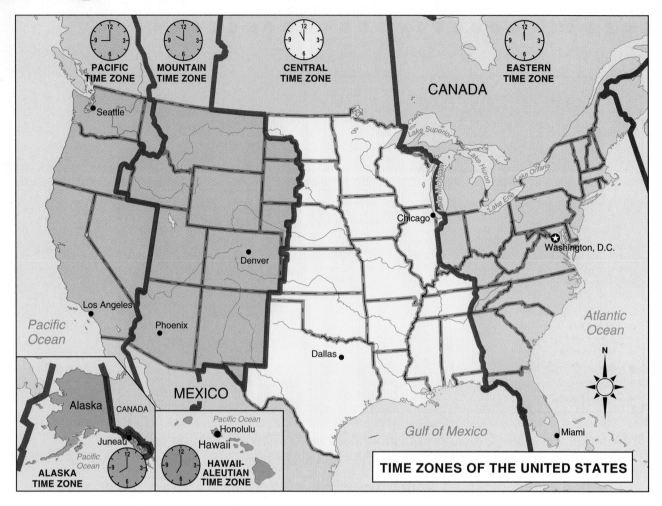

TIME ZONES OF THE UNITED STATES

You know that the Earth is turning all the time. It makes one complete rotation or turn every 24 hours. Remember that the Earth gets its light from the sun. Only half of the Earth receives light at a time. As the Earth turns, one part of the Earth gets lighter while another part gets darker.

It is not the same time everywhere on Earth. The Earth is divided into 24 time zones. There is one time zone for each hour in the day.

Six of the world's 24 **time zones** are in the United States. Look at the time zone map above. The time in each zone is different by one hour from the zone next to it. Washington, D.C. is in the Eastern Time Zone. Chicago is in the Central Time Zone. When it is 8:00 A.M. in Washington, D.C., it is 7:00 A.M. in Chicago. In Denver, which is in the Mountain Time Zone, it is 6:00 A.M. In San Francisco, which is in the Pacific Time Zone, it is 5:00 A.M. In the Alaska Time Zone, it is 4:00 A.M. In the Hawaii-Aleutian Time Zone, it is 3:00 A.M.

▶ In which time zone do you live? **Answers will vary according to location.**

▶ How do you think the Pacific Time Zone got its name? **The zone borders the Pacific Ocean.**

▶ What mountain range goes through the Mountain Time Zone? **Rocky Mountains**

▶ New York City is in which time zone? **Eastern**

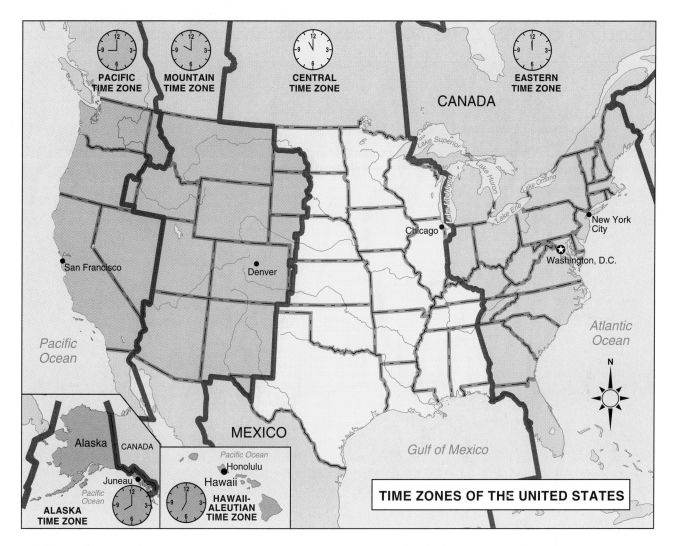

TIME ZONES OF THE UNITED STATES

If you know the time in one time zone, you can find the time in others. If you go east one time zone, add one hour to the time. If you go east two time zones, add two hours to the time. If you go west one time zone, subtract one hour from the time.

Look at the time zone map above. Put your finger on the Mountain Time Zone. Suppose it is 7:00 there. Move your finger one time zone east, to the Central Time Zone. Add one hour to the time. It is 8:00 Central time.

Move your finger back to the Mountain Time Zone. It is still 7:00. Now move your finger one time zone west to the Pacific Time Zone. Remember, you subtract one hour for each time zone you go west.

► What time is it in the Pacific Time Zone? **6:00**

► Name two cities in each time zone. **Pacific: Seattle, Los Angeles; Mountain: Denver, Phoenix; Central: Chicago, Dallas; Eastern: Washington, D.C., Miami**

► If it is 6:00 in Chicago, what time is it in Washington, D.C.? **7:00**
  What time is it in Phoenix? **5:00**
  What time is it in Seattle? **4:00**

► If it is 12:00 noon in Chicago, what time is it in Washington, D.C.? **1:00 P.M.**
  What time is it in Honolulu? **8:00 A.M.**
  What time is it in Juneau? **9:00 A.M.**

Reading a Time Zone Map

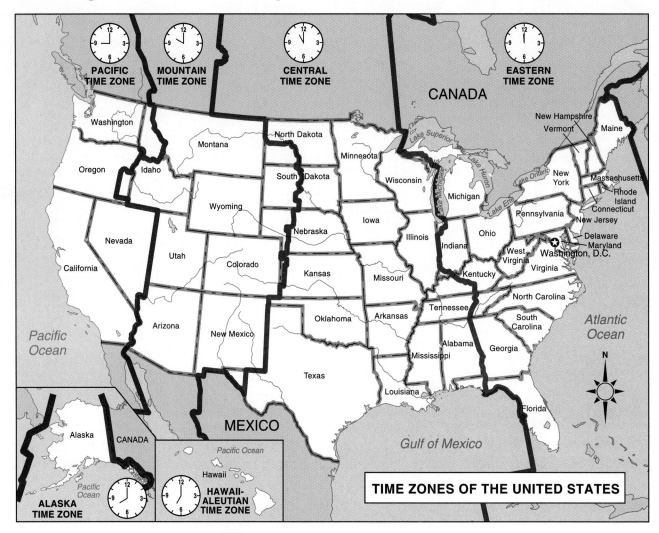

1. Lightly color the time zones. Use a different color for each zone. Notice that the lines are not always straight. Time zones often follow state boundaries or physical features. **Colored to match the directions**

2. In which time zone do you find these states?

California ____**Pacific**____   Pennsylvania ____**Eastern**____

Illinois ____**Central**____   Hawaii ____**Hawaii-Aleutian**____

3. It is 10:00 A.M. in California. What time is it in Wyoming? ___**11:00 A.M.**___

4. It is 5:00 P.M. in Georgia. What time is it in Alaska? ___**1:00 P.M.**___

5. It is 12:00 noon in Illinois. What time is it in Virginia? ___**1:00 P.M.**___

6. It is 4:00 P.M. in Massachusetts. What time is it in Oklahoma? __**3:00 P.M.**__

7. It is 12:00 midnight in Iowa. What time is it in New Mexico? __**11:00 P.M.**__

8. It is 4:30 A.M. in Colorado. What time is it in Washington state? __**3:30 A.M.**__

Reading a Time Zone Map

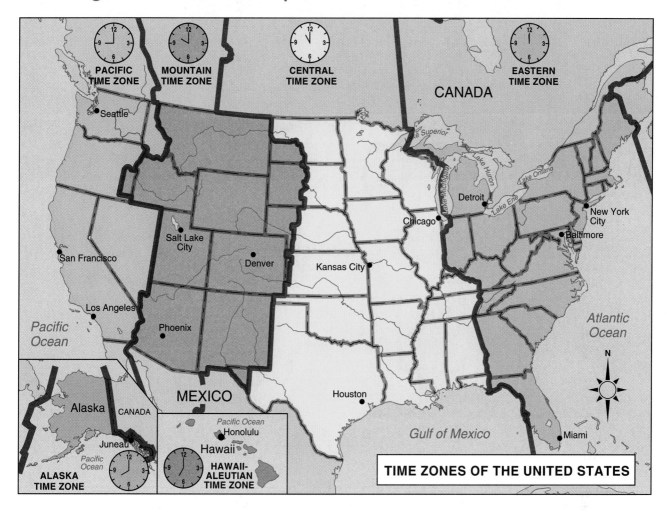

TIME ZONES OF THE UNITED STATES

1. It is 7:00 A.M. in Denver. What time is it in the cities listed below?

Honolulu	4:00 A.M.	Phoenix	7:00 A.M.
Los Angeles	6:00 A.M.	Miami	9:00 A.M.
Detroit	9:00 A.M.	New York City	9:00 A.M.

2. It is 12:00 noon in Chicago. What time is it in the cities listed below?

Juneau	9:00 A.M.	Seattle	10:00 A.M.
Denver	11:00 A.M.	Baltimore	1:00 P.M.
Houston	12:00 noon	San Francisco	10:00 A.M.

3. The first people to see the sunrise live in the ___Eastern___ Time Zone.

4. The last people to see the sun set live in the ___Hawaii-Aleutian___ Time Zone.

Reading a Time Zone Map

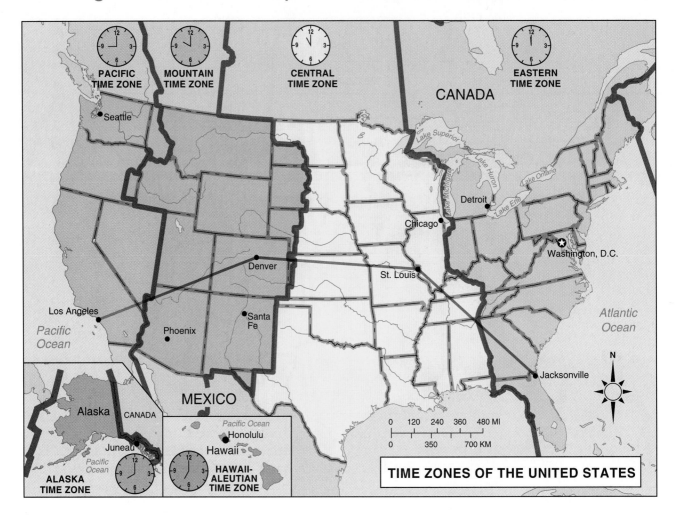

1. You will be traveling to several cities in the United States. Draw a line from Jacksonville to St. Louis. What direction will you be traveling? __northwest__ When you arrive in St. Louis, it is 2:00 P.M. What time is it in Jacksonville? __3:00 P.M.__

2. From St. Louis, you will drive to Denver. Draw a line to connect these two cities. From St. Louis to Denver is about __850__ miles. What direction will you be traveling? __west__

3. You will drive from Denver to Los Angeles to visit friends. Draw a line connecting these two cities.

   It is 7:00 A.M. in Los Angeles. What time is it in Denver? __8:00 A.M.__

   What time is it in Jacksonville? __10:00 A.M.__

Skill Check

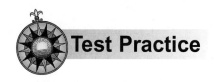
Test Practice

Vocabulary Check   time zone

Map Check

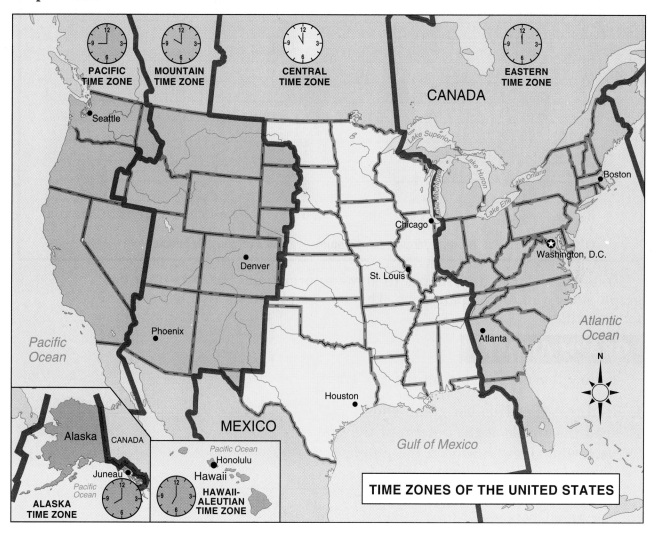

TIME ZONES OF THE UNITED STATES

1. The Earth is divided into 24 _____**time zones**_____ .

2. Atlanta is in the _____**Eastern**_____ Time Zone.

3. Phoenix is in the _____**Mountain**_____ Time Zone.

4. It is 2:00 P.M. in St. Louis. What time is it in the following cities?

   Denver ____**1:00 P.M.**____   Seattle ____**12:00 noon**____

   Atlanta ____**3:00 P.M.**____   Honolulu ____**10:00 A.M.**____

5. It is 12:00 noon in Denver. What time is it in the following cities?

   Houston ____**1:00 P.M.**____   Seattle ____**11:00 A.M.**____

   Juneau ____**10:00 A.M.**____   Washington, D.C. ____**2:00 P.M.**____

12 🌐 Graphs

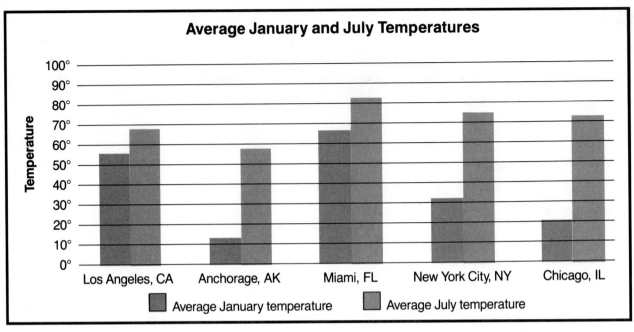

Average January and July Temperatures

Graphs use colors and shapes to show information. The bars on a **bar graph** allow you to compare facts. This bar graph shows two temperatures for five cities.

GRAPH ATTACK!

Follow these steps to read the bar graph.

1. Read the title. This bar graph shows ___average January and July temperatures___.
2. Read the words at the bottom of the graph.
   Name the cities shown on the graph.

   ___Los Angeles, Anchorage, Miami, New York City, Chicago___

   The green bars stand for ___average January temperature___.

   The orange bars stand for ___average July temperature___.
3. Read the words and numbers on the left side of the graph. The

   numbers on the graph stand for ___temperature___.
4. Compare the bars. Put your finger at the top of the first bar for Miami. Slide your finger to the left. Read the number there.

   The average January temperature in Miami is about ___67°___.

   The average July temperature in Miami is about ___83°___.

   Which city has the lowest January temperature? ___Anchorage___
5. Draw a conclusion. Which three cities have the coldest winters?

   ___Anchorage, New York City, and Chicago___

Reading a Bar Graph

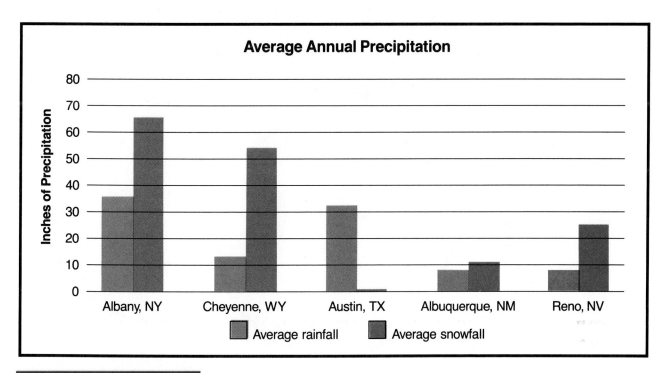

Average Annual Precipitation

Inches of Precipitation

80 70 60 50 40 30 20 10 0

Albany, NY   Cheyenne, WY   Austin, TX   Albuquerque, NM   Reno, NV

☐ Average rainfall   ■ Average snowfall

GRAPH ATTACK!

Follow these steps to read the bar graph.

1. Read the title. This bar graph shows __average annual precipitation__.
2. Read the words at the bottom of the graph.

   The brown bars on this graph stand for __average rainfall__.

   The blue bars on this graph stand for __average snowfall__.
3. Read the words and numbers at the left side of the graph.

   The numbers on the graph stand for __inches of precipitation__.
4. Compare the bars. Use more or less in each sentence.

   Cheyenne receives __less__ snow than Albany.

   Austin receives __more__ rain than Albuquerque.

   Reno receives __more__ snow than Albuquerque.

   Which city receives the most rain? __Albany__

   Which city receives the least snow? __Austin__
5. Finish the graph. Reno, Nevada receives 8 inches of rain. Add a bar showing the amount of rain Reno receives.
6. Draw a conclusion. Which city gets about the same amount of rain

   as snow? __Albuquerque__

Circle Graphs

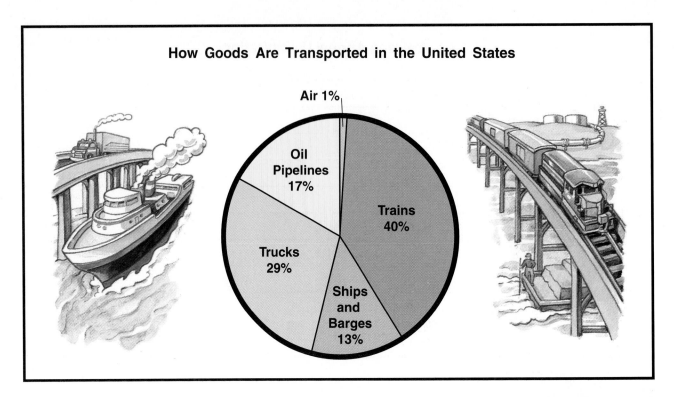

How Goods Are Transported in the United States

Air 1%

Oil Pipelines 17%

Trains 40%

Trucks 29%

Ships and Barges 13%

A **circle graph** shows the parts that make up a whole set of facts. Each part of the circle is a percentage of the whole. All the parts together equal 100%. This circle graph shows the percentage of all goods moved by each method of transportation.

GRAPH ATTACK!

Follow these steps to read the circle graph.

1. Read the title. The whole circle shows _____
   how goods are transported in the United States.

2. Read each part of the circle. Each part of the circle stands for a different way of transporting goods. What are the different ways?
   trains, trucks, oil pipelines, ships and barges, and air

3. Compare the parts. Read clockwise around the circle from the biggest part. Write More or Fewer in each sentence.

   _____**More**_____ goods are carried by trucks than by ships and barges.

   _____**Fewer**_____ goods are carried by trucks than by trains.

   _____**More**_____ goods are carried by trains than by oil pipelines and ships and barges together.

4. Draw a conclusion. What two methods of transportation carry about the same amount of goods? _____**oil pipelines and ships and barges**_____

Reading a Circle Graph

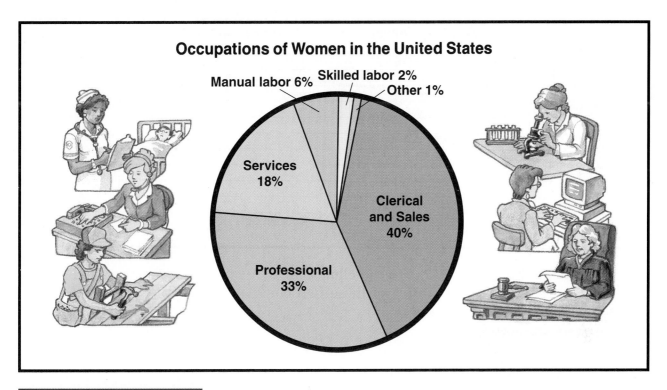

Occupations of Women in the United States

Manual labor 6% Skilled labor 2%
Other 1%

Services 18%

Clerical and Sales 40%

Professional 33%

GRAPH ATTACK!

Follow these steps to read the circle graph.

1. <u>Read the title.</u> The circle graph shows _occupations of women in the U.S._
2. <u>Read each part of the circle.</u>

   What percent of women hold clerical and sales positions? ___40%___

   What percent of women hold manual labor positions? ___6%___

   What percent of women hold positions in manual and skilled labor? _8%_
3. <u>Compare the parts of the circle.</u> Use <u>More</u> or <u>Fewer</u> in each sentence.

   ___Fewer___ women hold positions in skilled labor than in manual labor.

   ___Fewer___ women hold professional positions than clerical and sales positions.

   ___Fewer___ women hold professional positions than clerical and sales positions.

   Would you be more likely to meet a woman who was a professional or a woman who was in services? ___a professional___
4. <u>Draw a conclusion.</u> Most women work in what three areas?

   ___clerical and sales, professional, and services___

Line Graphs

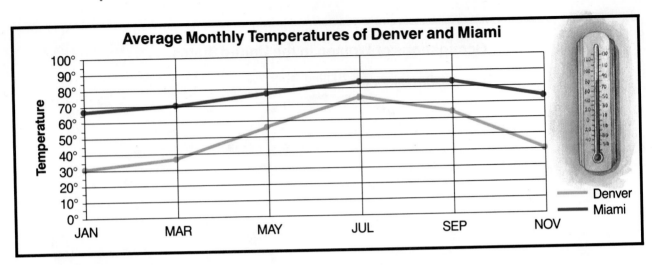

Average Monthly Temperatures of Denver and Miami

Some students wanted to compare the climate of two U.S. cities. They made a line graph to show the temperatures of these two cities. A **line graph** shows how something changes over time.

GRAPH ATTACK!

Follow these steps to read a line graph.

1. Read the title. This line graph shows _____ average monthly temperatures of Denver and Miami _____ .

2. Read the words along the bottom of the graph.
   This line graph shows the average temperatures for the months of _____ January, March, May, July, September, and November _____ .

3. Read the words and numbers on the left side of the graph. These numbers stand for _____ temperature _____ . The highest number is __100°__ .

4. Read the lines on the graph.
   Find the line for Miami. Put your finger on the dot above January. Slide your finger to the left and read the temperature.

   In January the average temperature in Miami is about __67°__ .

   In January the average temperature in Denver is __30°__ .

5. Compare the lines.
   Which city has the hottest summer temperatures? __Miami__

   Which city has the coldest temperatures? __Denver__

6. Draw a conclusion.

   Which city's temperatures change the least over the year? __Miami__

   How do you know? Answers will vary but may include: Denver's temperatures change more with the seasons than Miami's, as shown in a line that is not as even as Miami's.

Reading a Line Graph

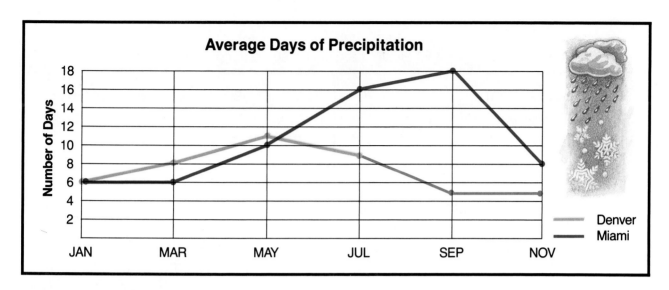

Average Days of Precipitation

Denver
Miami

GRAPH ATTACK!

Follow the first three steps on page 88 to begin reading this line graph.

1. <u>Trace the line for Miami with your finger.</u> Put your finger at the highest point on the line.

   What month does the dot stand for? _____ **September** _____

   How many days of precipitation did Miami have in that month? __ **18** __

   How many days of precipitation did Miami have in May? _____ **10** _____
   In what two months did Miami have the same number of days of

   precipitation? _____ **January and March** _____

2. <u>Finish the graph.</u> Finish the line for Denver. Add dots for this information. Then complete the line.

          September 5 days   November 5 days

3. <u>Compare the lines.</u>

   Which city had more days of precipitation in July? _____ **Miami** _____

   Which city had more days of precipitation in May? _____ **Denver** _____

   Which city had fewer days of precipitation in November? _____ **Denver** _____
   In what month did Miami and Denver have the same number of days of

   precipitation? _____ **January** _____

4. <u>Draw a conclusion.</u> Which city had the biggest change in number of days of

   precipitation overall? _____ **Miami** _____ How do you know? _____
   Answers will vary but may include: The line for Miami shows a greater difference in the number of days of precipitation than the line for Denver.

Tables

University Hills Bus Schedule							
WEEKDAY & SATURDAY SERVICE							
OUTBOUND from downtown (Bus sign reads AIRPORT)				INBOUND to downtown (Bus sign reads UNIVERSITY HILLS)			
5th & Congress	9th & Park	12th & Park	Airport & River Road	12th & Park	9th & Park	9th & Capitol	5th & Capitol
7:45	7:53	8:00	8:10	8:17	8:22	8:27	8:35
8:45	8:53	9:00	9:10	9:17	9:22	9:27	9:35
9:45	9:53	10:00	10:10	10:17	10:22	10:27	10:35
10:45	10:53	11:00	11:10	11:17	11:22	11:27	11:35
11:45	11:53	12:00	12:10	12:17	12:22	12:27	12:35
12:45	12:53	1:00	1:10	1:17	1:22	1:27	1:35
1:45	1:53	2:00	2:10	2:17	2:22	2:27	2:35
2:45	2:53	3:00	3:10	3:17	3:22	3:27	3:35
3:45	3:53	4:00	4:10	4:17	4:22	4:27	4:35
4:45	4:53	5:00	5:10	5:17	5:22	5:27	5:35

A **table** shows information using rows and columns. Tables put a large amount of information in a small space. This table is a bus schedule.

TABLE ATTACK!

Follow these steps to read the table.

1. Read the title. This table shows the ___University Hills bus schedule___.
2. Read the words at the top of the table.

   Where is the first stop? ___5th and Congress___

   When the bus is outbound, what does the bus sign read? ___Airport___

   What do the numbers in each column stand for? ___time of day___

   On what day could you not ride this bus? ___Sunday___

3. Read the table. If you caught the bus at 5th and Congress at 9:45, what time would you get to Airport and River Road? ___10:10___
   If you caught the bus at 12th and Park at 2:17, what time would you get to 9th and Capitol? ___2:27___
   If you needed to be at the airport at 12:30, what time should you catch the bus at 5th and Congress? ___11:45___
   If your plane arrived at 2:00, what is the earliest you could arrive at 5th and Capitol? ___2:35___

4. Draw a conclusion. Where does the bus make a loop and head back toward downtown? ___at Airport and River Road___

Reading a Table

Road Mileages Between U.S. Cities							
Cities	Birmingham	Boston	Buffalo	Chicago	Cleveland	Dallas	Denver
Boston, MA	1,215	—	461	1,003	654	1,819	2,004
Chicago, IL	667	1,003	545	—	346	936	1,015
Dallas, TX	647	1,819	1,393	936	1,208	—	887
Denver, CO	1,356	2,004	1,546	1,015	1,347	887	—
Detroit, MI	734	751	(277)	283	171	1,218	1,284
Kansas City, MO	753	1,427	995	532	806	554	603
Los Angeles, CA	2,092	(3,046)	2,512	2,042	2,374	1,446	1,029
Miami, FL	812	1,529	1,425	1,382	1,250	1,367	2,069
Minneapolis, MN	1,079	1,417	958	409	760	999	924
New Orleans, LA	351	1,563	1,254	935	1,070	(525)	1,409
New York, NY	985	215	400	797	466	1,589	1,799
Philadelphia, PA	897	321	414	768	437	1,501	1,744
Salt Lake City, UT	1,868	2,395	1,936	1,406	1,738	1,410	531
San Francisco, CA	2,472	3,135	2,677	2,146	2,478	1,827	1,271
Washington, DC	758	458	384	695	370	1,362	1,686

TABLE ATTACK!

Follow these steps to read the table.

1. Read the title.

   This table shows ___road mileages between U.S. cities___.

2. Read the words at the top of the table. What cities are listed across the top? ___Birmingham, Boston, Buffalo, Chicago, Cleveland, Dallas, Denver___

3. Read the words at the left of the table. How many cities are listed? __15__

4. Read the table. Put your finger on Boston at the left of the table. Slide your finger to the right until you come to the number under Chicago. Read that number.

   The distance from Boston to Chicago is ___1003___ miles.

5. Finish the table. Add these distances.

   Detroit to Buffalo   277 miles
   Los Angeles to Boston   3,046 miles
   New Orleans to Dallas   525 miles

6. Draw a conclusion. Which of the cities listed is farthest from Dallas?

   ___Boston___

THE WORLD

0   1000   2000 MI

0   1000   2000   3000 KM

180°   160°W   140°W   120°W   100°W   80°W   60°W   40°W   20°

80°N

Bering Sea

60°N

Hudson
Bay

NORTH

Great
Lakes

Rocky Mountains

AMERICA

Mississippi River

Appalachian Mountains

40°N

Atlantic Ocean

Tropic of Cancer

Gulf of
Mexico

20°N

Caribbean
Sea

Pacific Ocean

Andes

Amazon River

Equator

SOUTH

0°

AMERICA

20°S

Tropic of Capricorn

N

Andes

40°S

60°S

Antarctic Circle

80°S
180°   160°W   140°W   120°W   100°W   80°W   60°W   40°W   20°

EUROPE
ASIA
AFRICA
AUSTRALIA
ANTARCTICA

Arctic Circle
Ural Mountains
Ob River
Volga River
Danube River
Black Sea
Caspian Sea
Mediterranean Sea
The Himalaya
Ganges River
Red Sea
Nile River
Congo River
Arabian Sea
Indian Ocean
Pacific Ocean
Great Dividing Range

80°N
60°N
40°N
20°N
0°
20°S
40°S
60°S
80°S

40°E 60°E 80°E 100°E 120°E 140°E 160°E 180°
40°E 60°E 80°E 100°E 120°E 140°E 160°E 180°

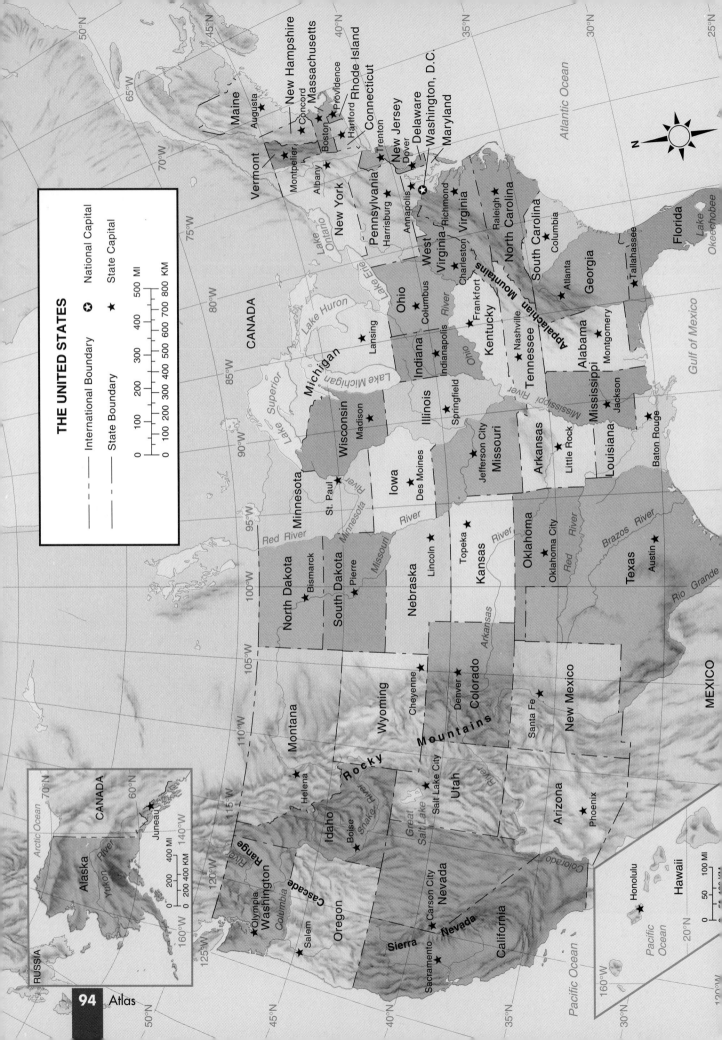

THE UNITED STATES

International Boundary
State Boundary

⊛ National Capital
★ State Capital

0 100 200 300 400 500 MI
0 100 200 300 400 500 600 700 800 KM

CANADA

Maine
Augusta
New Hampshire
Concord
Massachusetts
Boston
Providence
Rhode Island
Hartford
Connecticut
New Jersey
Trenton
Dover
Delaware
Washington, D.C.
Maryland
Vermont
Montpelier
Albany
New York
Pennsylvania
Harrisburg
Annapolis
Richmond
Virginia
Raleigh
North Carolina
Columbia
South Carolina
Florida
Lake Okeechobee

Lake Ontario
Lake Erie
Lake Huron
Ohio
Columbus
West Virginia
Charleston
Frankfort
Kentucky
Nashville
Tennessee
Atlanta
Georgia
Tallahassee
Appalachian Mountains

Lake Superior
Michigan
Lansing
Lake Michigan
Wisconsin
Madison
Illinois
Springfield
Indiana
Indianapolis
Ohio River
Mississippi River
Alabama
Montgomery
Mississippi
Jackson
Gulf of Mexico

Atlantic Ocean

Minnesota
St. Paul
Iowa
Des Moines
Missouri
Jefferson City
Arkansas
Little Rock
Louisiana
Baton Rouge
Red River
Minnesota River
Missouri River

North Dakota
Bismarck
South Dakota
Pierre
Nebraska
Lincoln
Topeka
Kansas
Oklahoma
Oklahoma City
Arkansas River
Red River
Texas
Austin
Brazos River
Rio Grande

Wyoming
Cheyenne
Colorado
Denver
New Mexico
Santa Fe

Montana
Helena
Rocky Mountains
Utah
Salt Lake City
Great Salt Lake
River
Arizona
Phoenix
Colorado River

Idaho
Boise
Snake River
Nevada
Carson City
California
Sacramento
Sierra Nevada
Cascade Range
Washington
Olympia
Oregon
Salem
Columbia River
Pacific Ocean

MEXICO

RUSSIA
Arctic Ocean
CANADA
Alaska
Juneau
Yukon River
70°N
60°N
160°W
140°W
0 200 400 KM
0 200 400 MI

Hawaii
Honolulu
Pacific Ocean
20°N
160°W
0 50 100 MI

Glossary

absolute location (p. 76)   the specific address or latitude and longitude coordinates of a place

acid rain (p. 48)   a kind of pollution that people cause that mixes with water vapor and falls to the ground as damaging rain or snow

Antarctic Circle (p. 57)   the parallel of latitude 66½° south of the Equator

Arctic Circle (p. 57)   the parallel of latitude 66½° north of the Equator

axis (p. 70)   the imaginary line that goes through Earth from the North Pole to the South Pole. Earth spins on its axis.

bar graph (p. 84)   a graph that uses thick bars of different lengths to compare numbers or amounts

cardinal directions (p. 8)   north, south, east, and west

charts (p. 35)   facts shown in columns and rows

circle graph (p. 86)   a graph that shows how something whole is divided into parts

climate (p. 71)   the average weather of a place over a long period of time

climate zone (p. 71)   an area with a generally similar climate

compass rose (p. 9)   a symbol that shows directions on a map

degrees (p. 56)   the units of latitude and longitude lines

elevation (p. 37)   the height of land above the level of the sea

Equator (p. 56)   the imaginary line around the middle of Earth that divides Earth into the Northern and Southern Hemispheres

geography (p. 4)   the study of Earth, its features, and how people live and work on Earth

grid (p. 50)   a pattern of lines drawn on a map that cross each other to form squares

hemisphere (p. 56)   half of a sphere; half of Earth; the four hemispheres are Eastern, Western, Northern, and Southern

high latitudes (p. 71)   the areas north of the Arctic Circle and south of the Antarctic Circle. These areas receive the least of the sun's heat.

human/environment interaction (pp. 5, 48)   the ways that the environment affects people and people affect the environment

human features (p. 4)   features of a place made by people, such as airports, buildings, highways, businesses, parks, and playgrounds

inset map (p. 23)   a small map within a larger map

interdependence (p. 34)   how people depend on one another to meet their needs and wants

intermediate directions (p. 9)   northeast, southeast, southwest, northwest

international boundary (p. 14)   where one country ends and another begins

interstate highway (p. 28)   a main highway that crosses the entire country

kilometers (p. 22)   a unit of length used in measuring distance in the metric system. Kilometers can also be written **KM** and km.

latitude (p. 56)   the distance north or south of the Equator measured in degrees

legend (p. 14)   a map key, or list of symbols on a map and what they stand for

line graph (p. 88)   a graph that shows how something changes over time

location (pp. 4, 76)   the absolute and relative position of people and places on Earth

longitude (p. 64)   the distance east or west of the Prime Meridian, measured in degrees

low latitudes (p. 71)   the area between the Tropic of Capricorn and Tropic of Cancer, which receives most of the sun's heat

map index (p. 51)   the alphabetical list of places on a map with their grid squares

map scale (p. 22)   the guide that shows what distances on a map equal in the real world

meridians (p. 64)   lines of longitude

middle latitudes (p. 71)   the areas between the Tropic of Cancer and the Arctic Circle and Tropic of Capricorn and the Antarctic Circle. These areas are warm in the summer and cool in winter.

mileage markers (p. 29)   small triangles and numbers on a map used to indicate distances along highways

miles (p. 22)   a unit of length that can also be written **MI** or mi

mountain range (p. 36)   a group or chain of mountains

movement (pp. 6, 34)   how and why people, goods, information, and ideas move from place to place

North Pole (p. 8)   the point farthest north on Earth

parallels (p. 56)   lines of latitude

physical features (p. 4)   natural features of a place, such as climate, landforms, soil, bodies of water, and plants and animals

physical map (p. 37)   a map that shows elevation and relief

place (pp. 4, 20)   physical and human features that make a location different from any other

plain (p. 36)   a large area of flat land

political map (p. 15)   a map that shows the boundaries separating states and countries

population map (p. 43)   a map that shows the number of people living in an area

Prime Meridian (p. 64)   the line of longitude from the North Pole to the South Pole and marked 0°. It helps divide Earth into the Eastern and Western Hemispheres.

regions (pp. 7, 29, 62)   places that share one or more features

relative location (p. 76)   describes a location by telling what it is near or what is around it

relief map (p. 36)   a map that shows the land on Earth

resource map (p. 43)   a map that uses symbols to show things in nature that people can use, such as coal, oil, and gold

rotation (p. 70)   the movement Earth makes as it spins around its axis

route (p. 28)   a road or path from one place to another, such as a trail, highway, railroad, or waterway

scenic road (p. 28)   a road that goes through beautiful areas

sea level (p. 37)   the level of the ocean surface

South Pole (p. 8)   the point farthest south on Earth

special purpose map (p. 42)   a map that gives information about a specific subject, such as climate, people, resources, or history

state boundary (p. 14)   where one state ends and another begins

state highway (p. 28)   a main road that connects cities and towns within the boundaries of one state

symbol (p. 14)   a picture on a map that stands for something real

table (p. 90)   a way of showing a large amount of information in a small space, using rows and columns

temperature map (p. 43)   a map that shows temperatures for an area

themes (p. 4)   main topics

time zone (p. 78)   an area on Earth where the time is the same. Earth is divided into 24 time zones.

title (p. 15)   the name of a map

Tropic of Cancer (p. 57)   the parallel of latitude 23½° north of the Equator

Tropic of Capricorn (p. 57)   the parallel of latitude 23½° south of the Equator